HappyStomach Cookbook

for DIABETICS

Food Is Our Highest Medicine

Jan London

HappyStomach Cookbook
for DIABETICS

Food Is Our Highest Medicine

Artwork by Jill Karlin Butler

Future Books
The author is planning a series of HappyStomach Cookbooks that focus on other common health conditions of our times.
The next book to be published is *HappyStomach Cookbook for the Recovering Alcoholic*.

North Atlantic Books has granted the author permission to use excerpts from *Healing with Whole Foods: Asian Traditions and Modern Nutrition*. These excerpts have been referenced by the single asterisk*.

Published by Jan London
www.happystomachbooks.com

Cover and interior art by Jill Karlin Butler

Interior design by Silvia Shablico, Evelina Färberová and Gabriella Varga

Photographs by Grazyna E. Jasiewicz

ISBN 978-0-9758955-1-1

Disclaimer
The advice offered in this book is based upon the author's own experience and is not intended to replace a qualified healthcare professional. The author shall have neither liability nor responsibility to any person or entity that incurs any loss, damage, or injury caused directly or indirectly from information in this book.

ACKNOWLEDGEMENTS

I am grateful to the many people who helped me, directly and indirectly, through the process of writing this book:

★ To Paul Pitchford, author of *Healing with Whole Foods: Asian Traditions and Modern Medicine*, for his support and encouragement and for his invaluable contributions.

★ To Paul's publisher, North Atlantic Books and Frog Books, for generously granting me permission to use excerpts from Paul's book, which have been referenced by the single asterisk*.

★ To Minx Boron, Life and Business Coach, who guided me through the concept process with her creative genius and our illuminated brainstorming sessions.

★ To Peggy Monahan who kindly offered her professional editorial skills and keen advice at a most critical time.

★ And to all of those whose misconceptions and disinformation have inspired me to write this book.

*Dedicated to the creative spirit
within all of us.*

CONTENTS

Food is our highest medicine

Food is our highest medicine

When you are inspired by some great
purpose, some extraordinary project,
all your thoughts break their bonds;
Your mind transcends limitations,
your consciousness expands in every direction,
and you find yourself in a new, great
and wonderful world.
Dormant forces, faculties and talents
become alive, and you discover yourself
to be a greater person by far
than you ever dreamed
yourself to be.
—Patanjali—

Food is our highest medicine

AUTOBIOGRAPHY OF A DIABETIC

A Spiritual Awakening

"Keeping your body healthy is an expression of gratitude to the whole cosmos—the trees, the clouds, everything."
—Thich Nhat Hanh

was diabetic for the first half of my life, but I never knew until recently. Ironically, this discovery happened while researching the current causes and effects of diabetes for this cookbook. It was an epiphany! The reasons for all those myriad health problems I had had throughout my life suddenly became crystal clear. I am certain, had I not changed my eating habits and other lifestyle patterns, I would have developed life-threatening illnesses attributed to my blossoming diabetic condition.

★   ★

Like most other baby boomers of my generation, I was bottle fed and then raised on the Standard American Diet (SAD!). At that time, illness was rarely attributed to food and diabetes was considered only an adult condition. Warnings about the harmful effects of refined white sugar, refined flour, and refined oil were not addressed until many years later. But, by then, it was too late. People had already become addicted to the tastes of this modern diet and spoiled by their comfortable, no-fuss lifestyle. I was just a victim of the times.

My father, his six siblings, and his mother all had the acquired form of type 2 diabetes. The common link was their sugar addiction and subsequent obesity. Owing that I do not have the symptoms attributed to type 1 or type 2 inherited forms, gene mapping was not the cause. I believe that I inherited sugar addiction or sucrophelia, a close cousin to alcohol and drug addiction. It may have been inherited from my father or it could have developed spontaneously during my fetal stage, due to my mother's high sugar diet. Either way, the seed had been firmly planted and then nurtured onward by my first food—sugar-laced formula milk. It did not take long before the effects of this addictive taste became apparent:

I was born slightly underweight, due to my mother's diet, and from infancy onward I was overweight. [Low birth weight is a sign of a weak condition.] At age 8, my appendix was removed. This undoubtedly resulted from the bacterial growth of E. Coli that thrive in the moist condition created by sugar.

At age 16, I began passing gallstones, clearly a result of my oily diet.

Three years later, my gallbladder was removed. My team of doctors exclaimed that I was their youngest patient ever with this condition. Yet, I was given no dietary restrictions and so I continued to consume excessively the poor quality dairy, meats, and eggs along with the refined oils, sugar, and flour products I had always craved. [The gallbladder is the liver's companion for storing bile, which is needed to digest oil, and a stressed liver produces unhealthy bile.]

Although I was not diagnosed with hypoglycemia, I had many of the symptoms including constant hunger, sensitivity to light, cold hands and feet, lack of concentration, ringing in the ears, sweating, a craving for sweets, muscle cramps, chest pain, and temper tantrums. [Hypoglycemia, or low blood sugar, often precedes the onset of diabetes.]

Around age 20, the color of my eyes had turned from hazel green to brown. [This change was the reflection of my congested liver that was now over-loaded with cholesterol-laden bile.] *Update: After eating only whole foods for several years, my eyes returned to their normal, hazel green color.*

My periodontal problems were attributed to both my poor diet and smoking habit. Unfortunately, at that time, dentists and dental hygienists had not yet been educated about the link between diabetes and gum disease. [Excessive amounts of refined sugar encourage the growth of harmful oral bacteria and bone loss.]

The physician I consulted about my bulging thighs and waistline told me I had a low thyroid condition. However, the medication he prescribed was not the solution, and my weight continued to climb. [A sluggish thyroid is largely due to an iron deficiency while excess weight around the middle is a visible sign of a diabetic condition.]

At 32, I stopped menstruating. Because the test results were normal, my physician told me not to worry. He also mentioned that I could not conceive until my menstruation cycle returned to normal. This meant that after 14 years I no longer needed birth control pills. [The absence or abnormal stoppage of menstruation, called Amenorrhea, is attributed to the excess amounts of estrogen in the birth control pill. Excess estrogen increases cholesterol levels in the bile, which causes stagnation in the gallbladder, resulting in the formation of gallstones. I was fortunate, though, for long-term use of birth control pills is also attributed to liver, breast, and cervical cancer.] *Update: After several years on a whole foods diet, my menstruation cycle returned to normal.*

> *"And the day came when the risk to remain tight in the bud*
> *was more painful than the risk it took to blossom."*
> —Anais Nin

I believe that life is a spiritual journey and I had been sleep walking through it. Then, something deep within gently nudged me and I began to awaken. It was now 1981. The shift toward more conscious food choices had gained momentum and I eagerly followed the movement. At this time, I was a single woman living in South Florida. My mornings were spent at the beach uncomfortably exposed in a bathing suit. Those extra fifteen pounds on my 5 foot, 2 inch frame were embarrassing. I was desperate to lose weight and, since I had never been successful at dieting, a water fast seemed to be my only solution. A few years before, I had fasted on water for three days and lost five pounds. It was difficult, but the results were worth it. This time three days would not be enough. For seven days I would need a controlled and disciplined environment.

The fasting retreat I attended was led by a naturopathic doctor who was also a raw foods advocate. I lost a dozen pounds, quit smoking, and continued to eat only raw vegetal foods. Having come from a heavy meat diet, the balance of raw foods worked well for me. I was beginning to discharge years of toxins attributed to the chemical laden meats and diary, food additives, and other impure foods I had been consuming. Soon my health and my attitude began to improve. I was no longer hypoglycemic, overweight, or constipated and my cravings for sugar began to fade. I had boundless energy and swam and jogged every day. I was happy and inspired for my life had direction and purpose.

Then, one fateful day, I relented and allowed my sister to serve me a macrobiotic meal of miso soup and brown rice. This seemingly simple food spoke volumes. It did not just taste good; it felt good. After two years of eating strictly raw foods, I changed at that very moment. The raw diet had had a dramatic cleansing effect, yet I instinctively felt that my body was now ready for something else.

Eager to know more, I began macrobiotic cooking classes. It was immediately apparent that this was a conscious, nearly reverent approach toward cooking—from the choice of daily foods and careful attention to their cleaning; to the specific cut of each vegetable and the method in which it is prepared; even to the stirring of food in a spiral, clockwise direction; to the attitude of the cook. All these actions have purpose for they embody the spirit of the food, which then nourishes our body and mind. What I had scrupulously read in the books was coming to life here in the kitchen and gathering momentum from within. It touched my soul and I loved it more than I can say.

> *"Man alone, of all creatures on earth, can change his own*
> *pattern. Man alone is the architect of his destiny."*
> —William James

My passion to learn more about the healing power of foods led me to distant lands for twelve insightful years. For the first eight years in the Hong Kong, I studied macrobiotic philosophy in harmony with Taoist principles under the guidance of a master. It was during this time I developed my cooking skills and the intuitive ability to create balance and harmony in my dishes. As I learned, these elements are key to the healing power of foods and ultimately to our well-being. They underlie the fundamental Law of Nature, that of cause and effect: for every action there is an equal and opposite reaction. This includes our choice of foods. When these choices are encouraged by emotion such as a craving for sugar, the reaction creates disharmony within the body or sugar imbalance. To restore emotional balance is a personal choice for it requires intent and self-control. To restore physiological balance begins in the kitchen. By replacing the sentimental taste of refined sugar with the grounding quality and natural sweetness of whole foods, sugar cravings begin to fade along with other cravings such as animal foods and alcohol. It is a natural progression. When healthy food choices take priority in our life, we are no longer a slave to our emotions. This is true freedom, true happiness. In effect, by changing our eating patterns, we re-shape our destiny.

For the following year, I continued on my personal journey traveling widely throughout the Far East and Southeast Asia. I then went on to Europe for three years. In each country, I focused on their traditional foods and the intuitive ways in which the native cooks created balance and spectacular flavors in their dishes. It was in both fine restaurants and humble kitchens around the world that I recognized, by substituting local ingredients, I could adapt these same regional specialties to my own style of cooking at home.

> *"If your food tastes good then change is not a hardship; it is a joy." —JL*

I am certain you will love my recipes for they will capture all your senses by their spectacular tastes, sensual textures, dazzling colors, and memorable aromas. Above all, their restorative powers contain all the necessary nutrients to help counteract the effects of a deficient diet. This power underlies the Laws of Nature and is the guiding principle behind the wisdom of my recipes.

From personal experience, I understand that the emotional transition from refined foods to whole foods can be a challenge because refined foods are addictive. In the beginning stages, you may need to practice a little self-control. Yet this, too, is part of the healing process. Be patient and allow the foods to work their magic. It is a path of rediscovery and a most enlightening journey.

I wish you all a happy stomach and a happy life.

Jan

> *"A happy life is one which is in accordance with its own nature." —Marcus Annaeus Seneca*

Food is our highest medicine

PART 1 ~ THE ENERGY FACTOR

God said [to Adam and Eve]: *"See, I give you every seed-bearing plant that is upon all the earth, and every tree that has seed-bearing fruit; they shall be yours for food."*
—Genesis 1:29—

Diabetes type 2 is an acquired condition. It is due to a lack of energy attributed primarily to the over-consumption of REFINED foods, meaning foods that have no energetic or nutrient value. It is why the first sign is a feeling of fatigue.

The purpose of food is to provide energy to the body in the form of nutrition. We measure a food's energy value in calories while vitamins, minerals, and enzymes form the foundation of nutrition. Therefore, we want to eat foods high in energy, high in nutrient value. Food that provides no nutrition has no energy. This is the true meaning of "empty" calories. Instead of focusing our attention on the *quantity* of calories we consume, as we have been trained to do so, we will instead focus our attention on the *quality* of these calories and the nutritive value they provide.

CARBOHYDRATES

Sugar is the body's mains source of energy.

Our highest energy foods come from the sugar inherent in complex and simple carbohydrates. Carbohydrates are further defined as either *unrefined* or *refined*—a most significant, yet widely misunderstood difference. Let's take a closer look.

UNREFINED CARBOHYDRATES
are whole foods. The complex form includes the whole grains—brown rice (also red and black rice), millet, rye, buckwheat, oats, barley, wheat berry, teff berry, amaranth, quinoa, and corn; land vegetables; sea vegetables such as arame, hijiki, nori/laver, kombu/kelp, wakame, and agar-agar; and the legumes—beans, lentils, and peas. Unrefined simple carbohydrates are fruits.

The naturally occurring sugar in these foods is balanced with the proper minerals, vitamins, and enzymes. Due to this synergisitic effect, normal metabolic activity is maintained and thus our health. The high fiber content in these foods (especially in whole grains) regulates blood sugar by releasing sugar slowly into the bloodstream. Fiber is also a natural colon cleanser. From another perspective, because vegetal foods are 90 to 95 percent water, they are low in calories yet they provide all the energy our cells need to perform their many tasks. Still and all, though plant foods are healthy, overeating is not. Quantity changes quality.

Refined carbohydrates speed up cellular death.

REFINED CARBOHYDRATES

are the products processed from whole foods. The complex form includes white rice, the flours milled from whole grains and legumes, and flour products such as bread, bakery foods, pasta, pizza, and breakfast cereal; and canned and frozen vegetables. Refined simple carbohydrates are packaged fruit juice and the products processed from the sugar cane and sugar beet plants.

Grains—The milling of brown rice to white rice removes its hull along with its outer covering—or bran and germ, which contain virtually all of its nutrients and fiber. Without nutrients, the rice is less filling. For example, one would have to eat approximately three times more white rice than brown rice to feel full. Without fiber, the food is quickly absorbed into the blood stream causing a spike in blood sugar levels, which explains why refined carbohydrates have a higher glycemic load than unrefined carbohydrates. Likewise, unless stone ground, nearly all nutrients and fiber are removed during the milling of grain into flour while the chemicals that are added to create self-rising and/or to whiten the flour are foreign to the body and therefore toxic.

Fruit juice (packaged form) is essentially a concentrated form of sugar that is void of fiber and the supportive nutrients needed to digest and metabolize it. Research shows that fruit juices raise the odds of acquiring type 2 diabetes and obesity by up to 25 percent. In addition, the various chemical ingredients added to extend shelf life and to improve color and texture have now been implicated as a major contributing factor to diabetes and obesity. (Further explained below under The Toxicity Factor.)

Sugar—The first step in the refining process produces molasses, which still contains some valuable nutrients. The following steps produce first raw sugar (a misnomer), then turbinado sugar, then brown sugar, and finally white table sugar—the most nutrient and acidic food substance of all and, therefore, the most harmful. Without nutrients, the body must borrow nutrients from other parts of itself in order to metabolize the sugar and safely remove it from the body. For example, calcium is taken from bones and is never replaced (osteoporosis). A healthy body can digest and eliminate around 2 tablespoons of white sugar a day. Today, the average person consumes his or her weight in sugar, plus over 20 pounds of (HFCS) high fructose corn syrup each year.

The obese individual consumes a great deal more than his/her own weight. (Consider that one 12-ounce can of cola contains around 8 to 12 teaspoons of sugar.)

THE PANCREAS FACTOR

From the perspective of Eastern medicine and theory, the pancreas paired with the spleen encompasses all the other organs of digestion, which in turn affects our blood sugar levels and thus our ability to think and concentrate.

When refined carbohydrates are consumed regularly, the pancreas is the first organ to suffer. It produces the hormone insulin. Insulin allows glucose (the broken down form of sugar) to penetrate the cells. Without the action of insulin, the cells cannot produce energy. Insulin is also needed to help digest fat and protein. In its effort to meet an ongoing demand, the pancreas produces too much insulin, resulting in hypoglycemia (low blood sugar). Overtime, the pancreas loses vitality and thus its ability to produce either sufficient insulin resulting in hyperglycemia (too much sugar in the blood) or effective insulin, resulting in diabetes. Without sufficient insulin, the excess sugar glucose circulates in the bloodstream traveling to all parts of the body, but most of it goes to the liver where it is stored as glycogen (starch) for emergency when extra glucose is needed such as when exercising.

Blood sugar levels are measured in milligrams per deciliter (mg/dl). The normal level is 83 mg/dl or less; a normal fasting level is in the mid- and high- 70 mg/dl range. A pre-diabetic condition or metabolic syndrome is characterized by fasting blood sugar levels starting at 100 to 125 mg/dl although some diabetes specialists believe that 90 is a more reasonable starting level.

OIL/FAT

Oil/fat is the body's other main source of energy. (Oil is fat in a liquid state.) Because it is a concentrated source, only small amounts are needed by the body. For the diabetic, no more than 2 tablespoons daily is advised.

Vegetal oils are extracted from the seeds of the plant. The degree of heat used in this process determines whether the oil is unrefined or refined.

UNREFINED

oils are either stone pressed (no heat) or processed under relatively low temperatures below 160°F (70°C). These oils still retain many of their nutrients along with their original taste, aroma, and color. Oils that are "first cold-pressed" have not been filtered and may appear cloudy.

REFINED

oils are typically heated to temperatures up to 450°F (230°C). Not only are the nutrients destroyed in this way, the fat molecules are transformed into fatty acids (trans fats). These misshapen molecules are not part of our evolution and therefore upset the natural order of life's ongoing process. In addition to high temperatures, the processing method can include as many as 40 different steps including bleaching, deodorizing, and degumming and each process requires a variety of toxic chemicals. As a result, the final product has a clear color, weak taste, and weak aroma. (The so-called "natural" or non-hydrogenated margarines are typically processed with chemical solvents, preservatives, coloring agents, and other toxic ingredients.)

THE LIVER FACTOR

The liver is tied to all bodily processes. It is why many scientists believe it is connected to, or at least aware, of every disease or dysfunction that is happening inside the body.

The liver performs hundreds of vital functions necessary for the smooth flow of energy throughout the body. One of its main functions is to convert fat and its store of glycogen into nutrients and then release this energy into the bloodstream to fuel our billions of cells. A diet high in both refined oils and carbohydrates severely affects its ability to function. The effects produce a chain reaction: the liver becomes congested with oil; its functions become stagnated; and the excess glucose is instead converted to fatty acids (cholesterol), which are then released back into the bloodstream. These travel first to the most inactive parts of the body—stomach, breast, buttocks, and thighs—and are then distributed to organs such as the heart and kidneys. As the fatty acids begin to build up, the function of these organs start to slow down.

A visible sign of a diabetic condition is excess weight around the middle indicating that the liver is swollen and congested with fat. To get a true picture of diabetes, testing should therefore include cholesterol levels along with blood sugar levels.

THE TOXICITY FACTOR

Recent scientific studies show that refined fats and carbohydrates are not the only primary causes for the epidemics of diabetes and obesity. The biggest threat may be the toxic chemicals[1] used in the convenience foods and other lifestyle products that support our comfortable standard of living. From another perspective, we can say that the primary cause is the consumers whose growing need for such high-tech products encourages more industries to meet their demands.

PROTEIN

The residues of as many as 500 to 600 toxic chemicals may be present in this country's meat supply, according to the U.S.A.'s Food and Drug Administration.

Contrary to popular belief, protein is not the body's main source of energy. It is used only if there is an insufficient amount of carbohydrates or fats available. All we need is three to four ounces a day for normal activity. The average American eats about three pounds or forty eight ounces of (conventionally farmed) animal protein a day—meat, eggs, cheese, and other dairy by-products. This amount of fatty, cholesterol-rich animal food threatens the cardiovascular system while the toxic chemicals end up in the liver.

> *"Nothing will benefit human health and increase the chances for survival of life on earth as much as the evolution to a vegetarian diet."* —Albert Einstein

Alternatively, the plant kingdom offers us a generous variety of protein-based, alkaline foods that help balance the acidic effects caused by flesh meat and refined foods.

Legumes provide our main source of protein. Generally, they contain the same amount of protein as a comparable amount of meat, poultry, and dairy without the fat. Soy products such as tofu, miso, and tempeh

---

1 Sources: Healthandenvironment.org, theecologist.org; Resources: Bruce Blumberg, Ph.D., Professor in the Departments of Developmental and Cell Biology, Pharmaceutical Sciences, and Biomedical Engineering at U. California, Irvine; David O. Carpenter, M.D., Director of the Institute for Health and the Environment at SUNY Albany and Professor of Environmental Health Sciences at U. Albany's School of Public Health

contain 1½ times more protein than meat and three times more than eggs.

Seeds and nuts are a concentrated source of protein. Because they are also high in fat content, only small amounts should be eaten. The exceptions are the seeds amaranth and quinoa, which contain about the same amount of protein as meat.

Whole grains contain about half the amount of protein as a comparable amount of most fish and meat. However, whole grains are a more complete and easily digestible food due to the moderating effect of minerals, vitamins, and disease-fighting phyto-nutrients.

Micro-Algae supplements—The aquatic plants spirulina, wild blue-green, and chlorella are primal life forms that exist on the edge of plant and animal kingdoms. They contain the highest sources of protein as well as chlorophyll, beta-carotene (vitamin A), and nucleic acids of any animal or plant food. Because of their special concentrated form of protein, only small amounts (10 to 15 grams daily) can satisfy both the emotional craving and the body's need for animal protein.*

DEFINING PLANT-BASED DIETS

Vegetarians do not condone killing animals for food. A strict vegetarian diet is void of all animal foods; a lacto-ovo vegetarian diet is void of meat, but includes dairy products and eggs. (In theory, a vegetarian diet can be a healthy choice, but only if the individual discerns between unrefined and refined foods.)

Vegan diet excludes all forms of animal products.

Raw foods diet contains no cooked foods only raw, fermented, and sprouted plant foods.

Fruitarian diet consists of only fruit.

Macrobiotics is based on the maintaining a healthy (pH) acid/alkaline balance through a diet of unrefined regional plant foods, sea vegetables, sprouts, and fermented foods. Depending on the individual's health condition, small amounts of seafood or poultry may also be included.

THE QUALITY FACTOR: FARMING METHODS

The nutritional value of our plant foods is initially influenced by the methods used to farm the crops. Let's take a closer look.

CONVENTIONAL FARMING
Pesticides, herbicides, and other toxic chemicals undermine the vitality of the soil. Therefore, food crops grown on this soil do not contain the full supply of minerals, vitamins, and other essential nutrients required for optimum nutrition and health. And the animals and humans that consume these plants are subject to mineral deficient diets. Taste is built upon carbohydrate and mineral levels in the plant, and when they decline so does the plant's taste and aroma.

The average conventionally grown apple has 20 to 30 artificial poisons on its skin, even after rinsing. This is one example of the contaminant level in conventionally grown produce. (Washing produce can help remove chemical residues on the surface.) According to the Environmental Working Group (ewg.org), the following fruits and vegetables (in the U.S.A.) contain the highest levels of contaminant residues. They are listed in order from highest to lowest: apples, celery, strawberries, peaches, spinach, nectarines (imported), sweet bell peppers, potatoes, blueberries (imported), lettuce, kale/collard greens. The cleanest conventionally grown produce is listed from least to most: onions, sweet corn, pineapples, avocados, asparagus, sweet peas, mangoes, eggplant, cantaloupe (domestic), kiwi, cabbage, watermelon, sweet potatoes, grapefruit, mushrooms[2].

Our food's nutritional value is further undermined by scientific methods.

GMO
Genetically modified organism or just GM, is the technology of inserting genes from other species (including humans) into the cells of the host plant thereby creating new life forms with unknown consequences. It is now widely believed that food allergies are directly related to GM foods. For example, a fish gene is inserted into a tomato or strawberry to give the fruit longer shelf life. If you are allergic to fish, and you eat this GM tomato, it is very possible you will have an allergic reaction to that tomato. Research shows that products made with GM soy beans (tofu, miso, soymilk) and wheat are responsible for triggering allergic

2 Source: Taste for Life Magazine, August, 2009.

reactions, especially when overeaten[3]. Today, most all conventionally farmed soybean, corn, cotton, sugar cane, and sugar beet crops in the U.S.A. are genetically modified. Because the Federal Drug Administration has approved GM technology, GM foodstuffs are not required to be labeled. So most likely, you have already eaten GM foods without knowing. Meanwhile, the newest technology known as the "genetics era" produces milk and meat from cloned cows[4]. These foods may also be on your grocery shelves, but unless you ask, you will never know because they are also not labeled.

Common GM products
- Fresh produce: corn, tomato, beets, potatoes, alfalfa sprouts, soy beans

- Cooking staples: canola and cottonseed oils, rice, wheat, tomato sauce, baking goods, chocolate

- Animal products: meat, dairy, poultry, eggs, farm raised fish

- Processed Foods: (nearly all) convenience foods, condiments, salad dressings, juice, soda, chocolate, and baby food; frozen meals, heat and serve meals, meal mix, cookies, crackers, snack food; (GM) soy ingredients and products—hydrolyzed soy protein, (TVP) textured vegetable protein, which is actually MSG or monosodium glutamate, soy flour, soy oil (vegetable oil is mostly soy oil), soy lecithin, soy protein isolates (SPI), energy bars; canned tuna in oil; vitamins and prescription drugs

Ways to avoid GM foods:
- Read produce and food labels. When looking at a product label, if any ingredients such as corn flour and meal, dextrin, starch, soy sauce, margarine, and tofu (to name a few) are listed, there is a good chance it has come from GM corn or soy, unless the label clearly states "Non-GMO" and/or it is listed as organic.

- Look at produce stickers. The PLU code for conventionally grown

3 Resource: Genetic Roulette: The Documented Health Risks of Genetically Engineered Foods, Jeffrey M. Smith, Yes, Books!, 2003; Sources: naturalnews.com, mercola.com.

4 Resource: Professor Bob Goodman, former head of research and development at the biotech company Calgene, (creators of the FlavrSavr tomato, the world's first GM food.

fruit consists of four numbers, GM fruit has five numbers prefaced by the number 8, and organically grown fruit has five numbers prefaced by the number 9.

- Go organic.

ORGANIC FARMING

Our most sensible choice is to buy organic whenever possible or to purchase our produce from local farmers. This is why:

- Pesticides gather in the seed of the plant.

- Organic plant food is not bio-engineered, genetically modified, or irradiated.

- For a food crop to be certified organic, the soil must be at least three years (36 months prior to harvest) free of no application of synthetic fertilizers, pesticides, or GMOs. "Sustainable" refers to plants that are grown according to the same principles as organic, but are not certified by the government. (Because organic certification is very costly, it is beyond the means of many reputable organic farmers.) "Wild grown" indicates that the crops are not cultivated. They are gathered in the wild.

- The organic label on packaged foods indicates that at least 95 percent of the ingredients are organically produced; the remainder can be non-organic or synthetic. For a product to be 100 percent organic, the law requires that absolutely no synthetic or non-organic ingredients are included. The same as with USDA Organic label. Production processes must meet federal organic standards and be verified by inspectors.

- Fresh organic produce contains on average 50 percent more vitamins, minerals, enzymes, and other micro-nutrients than intensively farmed produce and 30 percent higher levels of antioxidants.

- More than one million children between the ages of one and five ingest in excess of a dozen pesticides daily from conventional fruits and vegetables[5].

---

5 Source: Taste for Life Magazine, August, 2009 (article by Lisa Murray)

- Supporting organic growers means fewer consumer dollars in support of large chemical corporations and their political affiliations. Vote every day with your food dollars.

- Organic tastes so much better.

Although organic may cost a bit more, you will be pleasantly surprised by how much money your will save at the checkout counter—not to mention on health care costs—when you prepare your meals from scratch instead of buying expensive, nutritionally-deficient packaged foods. Furthermore, if there is a high demand for organics, more farmers will be encouraged to meet this demand, and then prices will naturally fall.

For best price buy locally grown, seasonal produce.

THE EXERCISE FACTOR

Exercise creates energy, which raises the oxygen level in our cells. When our cells are oxygenated our blood circulation is stimulated. When blood circulates better then all organs function better. This in turn reduces stress on the pancreas thereby improving cardiovascular function and the body's ability to metabolize glucose. This is why people who are physically fit secrete less insulin than people who are less fit. Exercise is especially important for older adults. Moderate exercise (e.g. walking) has shown to improve glucose tolerance in older, healthy adults, even without any weight or fat loss[6], while for postmenopausal women, regular exercise (moderately to vigorously over four times per week) can cut their risk of diabetes in half[7]. On an emotional level, exercise relieves stress, which in turn diminishes the accompanying feeling of hunger. Find a form of exercise you enjoy and do it every day.

"Walking is a man's best medicine." —Hippocrates

---

6 Yale University.
7 University of Minnesota in Minneapolis.

Food is our highest medicine

PART 2 ~ THE BASICS

"We have all the freedom to use what nature gives us, but without taking more than necessary."
—Nele Kantule—

Part 2: The Basics

HOW TO SHOP

- For optimal health, choose seasonal produce that grows in your climatic region. In other words, unless you live in a tropical climate, eating bananas from Central America during cold seasons is way out of balance.

- Look for bright, crisp, firm produce to ensure the best flavor and nutrition.

- Select leafy green vegetables whose leaves are firm and vibrant green and the stems should be moist. Dry stems indicate old greens.

- When choosing a round vegetable such as an onion, select the one with the roundest shape.

- Look for the smallest size vegetables and fruits. Their taste is concentrated and thus sweeter. (Oversized produce is usually a result of chemically treated soil, which effects its taste.)

- Examine the color of brown rice kernels. All or most of should be tan colored. Green kernels indicate the crop was picked too early.

- When purchasing grains and legumes in bulk, make sure the bins are covered and free of bugs, and the store has a good product turnover. For packaged grains and legumes, check the "use-by" date.

- Look for legumes with smooth surfaces and bright colors. Cracked seams or dull wrinkled surfaces indicate dryness.

- When buying nuts and seeds in bulk, taste one first to make certain they are not rancid. If it has a bitter aftertaste, do not buy it. Also, whole nuts, as opposed to pieces, keep fresher longer.

HOW TO READ LABELS

A product's label is a marketing tool and clever marketing sells product. Follow these guidelines and shop wisely.

Ingredient list—Read this first. It reveals most of what is inside the package. The ingredients are listed by percentage in order of their decreasing weight. Most often, you will notice some form of sugar or artificial sweetener listed among the top three ingredients. You can then refer to the nutritional chart for their gram count.

Nutritional chart can be misleading—quantity does not necessarily reflect quality. The naturally occurring nutrients that have been removed during the processing method are often replaced with chemical imitations that have virtually no power or efficacy. According to Michael Potter, CEO of Eden Foods, *"All products fortified with vitamin C are derived from GMO's, while other minerals and vitamins carry toxic substances with them. It took me two years to find an unadulterated vitamin B12 because all of the vitamin B12 manufactured in America and Europe has preservatives in them. And the law now states that this information does not have to appear in the ingredient list."*

Low fat/fat free foods are often higher in refined carbohydrates with nearly the same amount of sugar as the product they are replacing. The reason sugar is added is to replace the fat in order to preserve the flavor. According to the Joslin Diabetes Center, many so-called "diabetic" foods that are labeled "sugar free" or "no added sugar" in fact contain sugar alcohols, which raise blood sugar levels. Because many people typically overeat "sugar free" or "no sugar added" foods, their blood sugar may be significantly elevated.

> Caveat Emptor: In particular, beware of hydrogenated or partially hydrogenated vegetable oil, enriched flours, whole wheat flour (purchase only unrefined stone ground flour), chemical sweeteners, fortified vitamins and minerals, coloring agents, and "natural" flavorings (a misnomer). Any word that ends in "ose" usually denotes a chemical sweetener. In general, the highest quality packaged products have the lowest number of ingredients. As a rule, if the list is long with unfamiliar words, do not purchase the product.

ALL ABOUT COOKWARE

The most efficient pots are thick-bottomed. They distribute the heat evenly and prevent burning over high heat. The following are your best choices.

Earthenware: A Japanese form of lead-free pottery made from clay that is fired in a large kiln at a very high temperature. Cooking in earthenware pottery is the world's oldest and most natural way of cooking.

Cast iron: Choose cookware without graphite coating. Because cast iron is a porous material, it requires seasoning before use. Seasoning creates a thin layer of fat and carbon over the iron that coats the surface and prevents sticking.
How to season: Wash and rinse the pan well with a vegetable brush and soap to get off any factory residue. Then dry it on the stove over medium heat. Never alllow it to drain dry. Now it is ready to be seasoned. Coat the inside and sides of the pan evenly with oil and place in the oven at 250–300°F. In 15 minutes, remove the pan and pour out any excess grease. Place back in the oven and bake for 2 hours. A well-seasoned pan is nearly stick-proof. For an old pan that is rusty or dirty with food, scrub it with a pad or brush until it is clean and rust-free. Once the pan is clean, season by the method above.
Being a reactive material, cast iron can have chemical reactions with high acid foods such as wine, lemon, vinegar, tomatoes, and spinach. The food will take on a metallic flavor and turn a blackish color. Acid foods stored in cast iron will have the same reaction.
Cast iron cookware does not need to be washed with soap. This removes the pan's seasoning. It should not be soaked or left wet, or put in the dishwasher.

Wok: Highest quality woks are stainless steel and cast iron. A wok cooks the foods quickly, thus preserving the nutrients.
How to season: Heat the wok on the stove over high heat. Add a small amount of oil. Then take paper towels and distribute the oil evenly all over the inside of the pan and up the sides. Let that thin layer of oil burn onto the surface. Repeat this process three or four times until the pan becomes black. Clean while the wok is still hot. Wipe with a paper towel or cloth, or use hot water and a stiff vegetable brush. Place on a medium flame to dry or towel dry. Give it a light coating of oil before storing.

Stainless steel: An iron alloy containing a blend of chromium and nickel. Choose only heavy-gauge stainless or surgical steel or heavy cookware with a copper bottom. It does not conduct heat well, which means the food does not cook evenly. To clean, use a natural bristle or nylon pad. Metal scouring pads or scrubbers leave tiny scratches on fine finishes that dull the finish and encourage foods to stick. Use a dishwasher only when the manufacturer recommends it. In addition, harsh detergents can pit stainless steel pans. Leaving pans to soak for a long time may damage the finish as well.

Waterless cookware: Made from multi-ply stainless steel, it contains a moisture seal designed to cook vegetables without water or oil and with less heat (thus is energy-efficient). Cooked in this way, the nutrients are preserved, which is apparent by the food's vibrant color and sweet taste.

Caring for Your cookware: All cookware requires special care. Other than cast iron, pans are easily damaged by excessive heat, particularly the non-stick pan; cooking over high heat will also severely shorten its life. Wooden utensils are best for all cookware as metal can easily cause scratches. Do not put wooden utensils in the dishwasher. They soak up water and detergent and eventually crack.

Cookware to avoid: Aluminum is not only a poor conductor of heat; it can also affect our health. When cooking with aluminum under high temperatures or when cooking very sweet or salty foods, harmful toxins are released and combine with the ingredients. Teflon and other synthetic materials contain toxic substances that react and/or chip off into the food.

PART 3 ~ PRIMARY INGREDIENTS

"As I see it, every day you do one of two things:
build health or produce disease in yourself."
—Adelle Davis—

Part 3: Primary Ingredients

Some of the following ingredients may be unfamiliar to you, but do not be alarmed or discouraged. Most are easily interchangeable with similar, more commonly found ones. If any of these products are not sold in your local markets, you can contact the sellers directly or purchase them online. Refer to the Resources chapter for product listings.

SPECIALTY PRODUCTS

Arrowroot, a starch made from a tropical root, is high in calcium. Used as a healthy substitute for (GM) cornstarch to thicken soups and sauces.

Kuzu (or kudzu) powder is a thickening agent, similar to arrowroot, made from the root of the kuzu plant that grows wild in many countries including the U.S.A. In the Orient, kuzu is prized as a medicinal remedy for soothing stomach and intestinal disorders.

Mirin is a slightly sweet cooking sherry made from fermented rice. It balances salty flavors and adds complexity to soups, marinades and sauces, and sautéed dishes. Purchase only organic, naturally fermented brown rice mirin.

Miso is a fermented paste made from beans (soy, chickpea, aduki) or grains (rice, barley), and salt. The longer the miso is fermented, the darker the color, the stronger the taste, and the more powerful are its healing qualities. It is high in protein, amino acids, and contains a trace of vitamin B12.* It aids in digestion and creates an alkaline condition in the body promoting resistance against disease. In the Orient, it is used to treat and prevent radiation sickness, to treat certain types of heart disease and cancer, and to neutralize some of the effects of smoking and air pollution.* Use light color miso in warm weather and darker colors in cold weather. Choose organic miso (or at least non-GMO) that is unpasteurized, aged, and made with unrefined sea salt. Store in a glass or ceramic container in the refrigerator.

Flavoring with miso—Miso is a live food and, therefore, should not be boiled; boiling destroys its fragile enzymes. Add at the end of the cooking process: blend with a little soup broth or water, then add back to the pot, and gently simmer for a few minutes to allow flavors to blend.

Sesame paste is made from both unhulled tan and black sesame seeds. (Sesame tahini is made from hulled sesame seeds.) Because it is high in fat content, use only small amounts. Both varieties are usually sold in Oriental markets or they can be purchased online (refer to the Resources section).

Shitake mushroom is different from other mushrooms because it is grown on oak trees and thus its woodsy flavor. It is an excellent source of B vitamins, vitamin D, magnesium, and iron. Available in both fresh and dried forms.

Shoyu is a naturally produced soy sauce made from fermented soybeans, wheat, and salt. Add at the end of the cooking process (otherwise, it loses its flavor), but it can also be used at the table.

Tamari is a wheat-free soy sauce made as a by-product of miso. Highest quality is made with only non-GM soy, salt, and water. It is a far more superior product than the mass-market brands that usually contain preservatives and food coloring. Tamari is high in amino acids and has a stronger flavor than shoyu. Unlike shoyu, it must be cooked into the food, not used at the table.

Tempeh, a product from Thailand and Indonesia, is a fermented food made from cooked soybeans. It is both an easily digestible form of protein and high in omega-3 oils. Its strong taste makes it a popular substitute for meat, poultry, and fish.

Tofu is made from cooked soybeans. It is high in protein, calcium, B-vitamins, potassium, and iron and low in fat and calories. Highest quality tofu is made with nigari, a natural solidifier. Avoid tofu that is solidified with alum, the chemical form of nigari. Because most soybeans are now genetically modified, purchase tofu made with either organic or non-GMO soybeans. The different textures of tofu are extra firm, firm, soft, and silken depending on how much water was extracted during production. Extra firm and firm are best for frying and sautéing; soft and silken are best for making sauces and dressings.

Umeboshi products are an ancient Japanese food reputed to be the most alkalizing foods on earth.
Umeboshi plum, a salty-sour pickled plum, is an effective, natural remedy to balance acidic conditions such as hangovers, food poisoning, and acid indigestion. Both the whole plum and the paste (made from the puréed pulp of the pickled plum) are suitable for salad dressings, beverages, spread on nori rolls and corn-on-the-cob, and more.

(Umeboshi concentrated paste and umi balls are strictly for medicinal purposes.)

Umeboshi vinegar is a by-product from traditional pickling of umeboshi plums. It is rich in organic acids and has a tangy and very salty taste. Use over cooked vegetables, with bean dishes, in salad dressings, and for pickling. Other medicinal benefits are described below.

Vinegar helps to balance salt and fat and to reduce cravings for strong sweets; in the Orient, vinegar is used to generate energy through the liver improving blood circulation.* Beware that many commercial vinegars are synthetic products made from glacial acetic acid, a petroleum product. Others are made from alcohol produced for industrial use. Avoid any vinegar labeled "distilled" as it is a most highly refined chemical, not food. I recommend brown rice, unrefined apple cider, umeboshi, and organic balsamic vinegars.

WHOLE GRAINS

Amaranth is an ancient Aztec food and a staple in parts of South America. Although it is prepared as grain, it is actually the seed of a flowering plant.* It specifically benefits the lungs and is high in protein (15–18 percent) as well as fiber, amino acids, vitamin C, and contains more calcium than milk.

Barley, in its whole form, is easily digestible and soothing to the stomach. The processing method of the "pearled" form removes many of its nutrients and thus its healing powers.

Brown rice strengthens the spleen and pancreas, soothes the stomach, expels toxins, and increases energy; it is concentrated in B vitamins and thus helps relieve mental depression or other symptoms of the nervous system.*

Mochi is a sweet brown rice that has been pounded and formed into a block. It is an easily digestible and strengthening food with a glutinous (texture) and sweet taste. The different varieties are plain, cinnamon and raisin, sesame, millet, garlic, and mugwort (an herb used to remove parasites).

Buckwheat nourishes the lungs, kidneys, and bladder; aids in eliminating water or fluid retention; reduces blood pressure; and increases circulation to the hands and feet. Because buckwheat is not part of the wheat family, it is a safe grain for those with wheat allergies.*

Corn helps regulate digestion, nourishes the heart, tonifies the kidneys, and promotes healthy teeth and gums.*

Millet, known as "the queen of the grains", is the most alkalizing of all grains; it balances over-acid conditions and is therefore the best grain for diabetics, alcohol abusers, and those with hypoglycemia; it strengthens the kidneys and benefits the spleen, pancreas, and stomach.*

Oats are truly a comfort food. The oats plant (or oat groats) has beneficial effects on our central nervous system. Various parts of the plant are used in traditional herbal medicine to treat depression, anxiety, exhaustion, and addiction. Oats are also known to remove cholesterol from the digestive tract and arteries; and strengthen cardiac muscles, the pancreas, and spleen.*

Quinoa (keen'wa) is closely related to amaranth with some of the same characteristics. It benefits the kidneys and, like amaranth, has more calcium than milk.* It is also higher in fat content than any grain and a good source of iron, B vitamins, and vitamin E. It has a sweet and bitter flavor. Its bitterness can be offset when combined with other grains, popped like popcorn, or roasted.

Rye cleans and renews arteries; its bitter flavor benefits the liver, gallbladder, pancreas, and spleen.*

Teff berry is the smallest of all grains and the staple grain of Ethiopia and Eritrea. It is believed to have originated in Ethiopia between 4000 BC and 1000 BC. Teff excels in regulating blood sugar levels and is especially high in protein and iron. It contains no gluten so it is appropriate for those with gluten intolerance and Celiac disease. Teff goes well with brown rice, millet, couscous, buckwheat groats, corn, amaranth, and quinoa.

Wheat berry targets the kidneys and nurtures the heart—calming palpitations and soothing stressful emotions; the over-eating of refined, rancid, and genetically modified wheat products partly explains the many common allergies to this vital food.*
Spelt and kamut are ancient forms of wheat that have not been genetically modified and usually do not cause allergic reactions in those who are gluten intolerant.*

OILS

Both the quality and quantity of your oil are paramount to your recovery. Because pesticides gather in the seed of the plant, choose organic and first cold-pressed oils whenever possible.

SPECIALTY OILS

Sacha inchi oil is extracted from a small peanut-like nut that grows wild in the jungles of Peru. It is high in protein and very digestible. The omega 3, 6, and 9 contained in it has the potential to lower HDL cholesterol when used in moderate amounts. Due to its recent popularity, the nut is now being cultivated. For best quality, purchase wild crafted sacha inchi oil.

Argan oil is produced from the nut of the argan tree, which is indigenous only to Southwestern Morocco. It is high in vitamin E and has been shown to significantly reduce cholesterol levels. Available both unroasted and roasted.

Pumpkin seed oil is a specialty product from the Styria region of Austria. Its deep green color reflects its unique, rich taste.* The seeds and its oil benefit the colon, pancreas, and spleen; specifically recommended for impotency and swollen prostate with signs of urination problems.*

Red palm and coconut oils are saturated fats, composed mostly of medium chain fatty acids. Coconut oil is about 80 percent saturated fat while palm oil (made from the fruit of the plant, not the nut) contains only about 40 to 50 percent saturated fat. Japanese experiments revealed that a certain fat cell hormone, adiponectin, plays an important role in preventing diabetes and arteriosclerosis. The types of medium chain fatty acids that have the property to raise the level of adiponectin in the blood are contained only in mother's milk and in coconut and palm oils. Because red palm oil contains both lower levels of saturated fat content and a higher content of adiponectin, it is a favored choice over coconut oil. The research group concluded that medium chain fatty acids can be beneficial in the prevention of obesity, but **only** in small amounts.

GUIDELINES

High temperature cooking—Red palm, coconut, and sesame oils can be heated to high temperatures (but never to the smoking point) without changing to a trans fatty acid.

Sautéing—The oils listed above along with olive, corn, pumpkin, grape seed, and argan oils.

Non-cooking—Flax, hemp, chia, and sacha inchi oils are specifically for non-cooking purposes.

OIL SCAMS

Canola is not natural oil; there is no 'canola' plant. Its name is an amalgam of the words "Canada" and "oil". Canola was developed in Canada from the rapeseed plant, which is part of the mustard family of plants. It was also the first genetically engineered plant. According to AgriAlternatives magazine, *"By nature, these rapeseed oils, which have long been used to produce oils for industrial purposes, are... toxic to humans and animals."* The plant is also naturally insect resistant because insects, intuitively, will not eat it.

Olive oil—There is more olive oil sold than there are olives grown. This is because olive oil is commonly adulterated with substances like refined hazelnut oil from Tunisia and canola oil. If an oil is blended with less than 15 percent other oil, it is still considered as "extra virgin". It is estimated that ninety per cent of olive oil sold in Italy as extra-virgin is not of premium grade. If the label does not say "Made in Italy", most likely it is not made in Italy. "Bottled in Italy" usually signifies that the olives are not of Italian origin. Best quality olive oil is organic, extra virgin, and stone pressed or first cold-pressed.

STORAGE

All oils are sensitive to heat, light, and exposure to oxygen. Proper storage will keep the oil from going rancid. (Rancid oil has an unpleasant aroma and acrid taste.) Also, fresh herbs that have been added to bottled oils can become rancid over time.

Store all oils in the refrigerator except for olive, coconut, and palm oils, which turn solid at temperatures below 76°F. Store these oils in a cool, dark place. Olive oil keeps at least 9 months after opening. Most other oils will keep around 8 months after opening. The exception is unrefined coconut oil. Unless cold pressed, it will keep around three months. To preserve freshness, store in the refrigerator and either use it as coconut butter or melt it before using. Unless specified on the label, all oils readily combine with most types of plastic to form toxic plasiticides. Therefore, purchase oils that are bottled in glass. Dark glass is best.

SALT

The salt content of our blood is very similar to sea water because we evolved from the sea.

THE QUALITY FACTOR

In its natural state, salt contains a full range of minerals that are essential for keeping us alive.

Unrefined sea salt ranges from slightly grey in color to white. Pink salt is hand-harvested from ancient volcanic sea beds. Various shades of pink are attributed to the different minerals in the soil. Natural salt is somewhat moist due to its power to attract water from air and therefore does not pour easily like the refined variety. Any salt that is not damp has an added chemical, which is not required to be identified on the label.

Refined sea salt: This is a fine, white grain. Many of its essential minerals along with its moisture are removed during the processing method. (Some companies list the added chemical ingredients on the package.)

Table salt: Nearly all of the sixty trace minerals present in its natural state have been replaced with dextrose to stabilize the added (synthetic) iodine, anti-caking chemicals, potassium iodide, and aluminum silicate. (Aluminum is a very toxic substance dangerous for the nervous system and has been found to be one of the primary causes of Alzheimer's disease.) Two of the minerals removed are magnesium and calcium. Calcium is needed for strengthening bones, nerves, heart and muscles, and for brain development. An imbalance of magnesium affects the kidneys and gallbladder making them more susceptible to the formation of stones. An imbalance also creates an incessant craving for salt that can lead to salt sensitivity, which is reported to be more common in obese and insulin resistant individuals.

THE QUANTITY FACTOR

When taken in small quantities, natural sea salt helps to maintain proper blood sugar levels in the body; has an alkalizing effect due to its broad range of minerals; aids in communication of brain cells; keeps the body well hydrated thereby boosting the immune system. Because salt helps food to digest faster, it can also benefit dieters: Quicker elimination helps to prevent buildup in the digestive tract. Undigested food can eventually lead to constipation, bloating, and thus weight gain.

Excess salt in the diet is known to be a cause of high blood pressure, ulcers, cancer of the stomach, and edema. Early signs of excess salt are unusual thirst, dark urine and complexion, clenched teeth, and bloodshot eyes.*

Insufficient salt in the diet also creates an imbalance in the body. Symptoms can be diminished strength and sex drive, intestinal gas, and vomiting.*

GUIDELINES

- As a rule of thumb, per day you need about three to four grams for every ten glasses of water or a quarter teaspoon of salt per quart of water.

- Use a pinch of sea salt on raw fruit for balance and to enhance its sweet flavor. Otherwise, cook with natural sea salt rather than adding it at the table.

- Other than grains, it is best to add salt towards the end of the cooking process.

- In cooking, salt should not dominate the taste of food. Use it to bring out the food's natural flavors.

- Most prepared foods contain a high salt content.

WATER

*"Roughly 40 percent of bottled water begins as tap water." —*Earth Policy Institute

Because water is an important ingredient in our recipes, quality matters.

Spring water: The purest waters come from very deep within the earth and are estimated to be thousands of years old. The various minerals that are extracted from the rocks and soil reflect its taste. When purchasing bottled spring water, choose water that has been bottled directly at the source and not at the processing plant. The source information is printed on the container label.

Distilled/Purified water: This essentially is refined water. It has no life force, no minerals, and, therefore, no taste. Cooking foods in distilled water tends to extract minerals, which affects the food's nutritional value. According to the U.S.A. Environmental Protection Agency, *"Distilled, purified water, being essentially mineral-free, is very aggressive, in that it tends to dissolve substances with which it is in contact. Notably, carbon dioxide from the air is rapidly absorbed, making the water acidic and even more aggressive."*

Rain/Well water: In theory, these are both good sources. However, because water is a very effective solvent, it picks up pollutants from the atmosphere and the earth. It is best to have the water tested for purity, and then filter it.

Filtering Systems: Most all municipal water systems in the U.S.A. contain varying levels of toxic chemicals including fluoride (a chemical by-product of aluminum, steel, cement, and phosphate). Therefore, it is necessary to use a filtering system. (Refer to the Resources chapter for the highest quality filtering systems.)

A reverse-osmosis process produces ionized water. As research has shown, ionized water alkalizes the blood, which is especially beneficial for those with diabetes and other acidic conditions. Reverse osmosis removes virtually all contaminants from the water, including fluoride, especially when combined with a pre- and post-carbon filtration system.

Water filtered through a solid charcoal filter is slightly alkaline. Ozonation of this charcoal filtered water is ideal for daily drinking. The system should be encased in high quality ceramic.

A counter-top or pitcher filter typically filters out only particulate matter, not fluoride or other chemicals.

SWEETENERS

RECOMMENDED SWEETENERS

Like oil, the quantity and quality of your sweeteners are vital to your recovery. The following natural sweeteners provide nutritional value and have a low glycemic index (less than 55).

Coconut water cleanses the kidneys and is helpful in treating edema resulting from diabetes and a weak heart.*

Fresh/dried fruit—Fresh fruit complements raw vegetable salads; ripe fruit or cooked fruit can be blended and added to sweeten desserts. The sugar content in dried fruit is highly concentrated, so use small amounts. The dried fruits apricots, dates, figs, prunes, and raisins work well in recipes. Rehydrate by soaking in very warm water until soft, and then purée with the soaking water for a sauce consistency. Purchase either organic dried fruit or fruit without added sugar or chemical preservatives.

Licorice root is high in B vitamins and minerals and is 50 times sweeter than sucrose with virtually no calories. It is sold in dried root form and as a gray-green, very fine powder. Licorice root combines well with allspice, cardamom, cinnamon, cloves, coriander, fennel seed, ginger, pepper, poached fruit, and poultry. When purchasing, look for deglycyrrhized licorice.

Stevia is a sweet tasting herb from the rain forests of Paraguay. It is non-toxic, alkalizing, calorie-free, and has a zero glycemic index. Like all other herbs, it contains minerals and vitamins along with medicinal qualities. The least processed forms and, therefore, the best choices are: the live plant; the dried cut leaves and leaf powder sold in bulk form; tea bags; and the dark liquid concentrate, a fermented food made from the fresh leaves. Its taste and color is similar to molasses.
A half-cup of sugar is equal to about one teaspoon concentrate and about one tablespoon dried leaves or leaf powder. Purchase leaves that are freshly dried.

Syrups are a concentrated sweetener, so only small amounts are needed.
A half-cup of sugar is equal to: 1/3 cup yacon; 1¼ cups rice syrup and coconut nectar; 1½ cups barley malt; and ¾ cup molasses. Unless specified in the recipe, use any of the following syrups:

Yacon syrup is processed from the root of the yacon plant, a mildly sweet tasting tuber indigenous to the Andean region of South America. The syrup is not only delicious; it is also a powerful medicine—it lowers blood sugar levels. For centuries, the native people have used its roots and leaves to treat diabetes, strengthen the immune system, and to help improve the health of those with chronic liver disease and kidney ailments. The syrup has a consistency between molasses and maple syrup and its taste and color are similar to molasses and caramel. *Caution: Not recommended for those with hyperglycemia.*

Barley malt is made from sprouted barley. Its flavor, color, and texture are similar to molasses.

Brown rice syrup, also called rice yinnie, is a naturally processed sweetener made from sprouted brown rice. It is has a light color and a mild, sweet flavor.

Coconut nectar and **Coconut sugar** are produced from "sap" collected from blossoms that grow on a certain type of coconut tree. The sap is cooked down to a syrup consistency called "coconut nectar". By further evaporating the syrup produces a crystal form called "coconut sugar." (If processed at or below 104°F, the product qualifies as "raw".)

Molasses (unsulphered)—Barbados molasses is made from the first pressing of sun-ripened sugar cane juice. It has a sweet taste and contains some vitamins and minerals. Black-strap is made from the final extraction process. It contains nutritional value and has the lowest sugar content, but it has a bitter taste. The sulphered variety is made from the immature plant, which has not reached sweet peakness. To speed up the sweetening process, it is commonly treated with sulpher fumes during production and is therefore not recommended.

SWEETENERS TO AVOID

Plant-based

Agave syrup is produced from the same plant family from which tequila is made. It is mostly chemically refined fructose (from 70 percent and higher). Fructose, like white sugar, converts to fatty acids in the liver, but more easily. ("Raw blue agave" is not a raw product. It is the product's name and a clever marketing strategy.)

Fruit juice concentrate lacks fiber and disease-fighting phytonutrients. Because it is a concentrated source of sugar, it is quickly absorbed into the bloodstream causing a spike in blood sugar levels.

Honey, in its raw unfiltered form, might have a few more vitamins (very small amounts of B vitamins and vitamin C), antioxidants, and enzymes than white sugar. However, it is highly refined by bees and is very quickly assimilated directly into the bloodstream. The refined variety has no appreciable nutritional value.

Maple syrup, unless unrefined and organic, may contain formaldehyde and other toxic chemicals[1]. If you must, then purchase a syrup that is organic, unrefined, and grades B and below.

Sucanut, sold as Sucanat, is a processed form of dried granulated (GM) sugar cane juice. Although it contains some complex sugars, vitamins, minerals, and amino acids, it is metabolized as sugar in the liver.

Synthetic

Over time, the following chemical sweeteners, commonly used by diabetics, lead to further liver congestion.

Aspartame, a product developed by Monsanto Company, is considered the most harmful of all sugar substitutes. (In 1985, the FDA's own toxicologist, Dr. Adrian Gross, told Congress, *"without a shadow of a doubt, aspartame can cause brain tumors and brain cancer."*) Its trademarks, NutraSweet, Equal, and Spoonful are used in over 9,000 products from vitamins and medicines to desserts.

Dextrose/Maltodextrin, also called corn sugar, is chemically produced from GM corn, potato, or rice.

Fructose is a misnomer and intentionally misleading. Unlike the naturally occurring fructose in some root vegetables and tree fruit, this form is derived from (GM) corn and thus its name, high fructose corn syrup (HFCS). While natural fructose is digested in the intestine, HFCS is processed in the body through the liver. Once eaten, it appears as triglycerides in the blood stream, or as stored body fat. Elevated triglyceride levels are building blocks for hardening human arteries. A Harvard School of Public Health Study concluded that those who drank one or more servings of HFCS sweetened soda or fruit punch a day for over four years, not only gained an extra ten pounds, but also ran an 80 percent risk of developing type 2 diabetes. It appears in medicines, vitamins, wine coolers, as an additive to formula milk, and much more.

---

1 Fields, M, Proceedings of the Society of Experimental Biology and Medicine, 1984, 175:530-537; Source: living-foods.com

Crystalline fructose, a close cousin to HFCS and the newest generation of artificial low-calorie sweeteners, produces basically the same harmful effects as HFCS. So far, it is used primarily in beverages and yogurt.

Sucralose, sold as Splenda, is a chlorinated sucrose derivative with fillers maltodextrin and/or dextrose. Common side effects can include stomach cramps and diarrhea.

Food is our highest medicine

PART 4 ~ THE COOKING PROCESS

"...no one is born a great cook, one learns by doing."
—Julia Child, My Life in France—

HEAT SOURCES

Fire is our best choice. Its powerful life force permeates the food, producing a superior taste and higher nutrition.

Electric heat changes the molecular structure of the food while radiant type heat cooks the food at an even higher vibration. In both forms, the taste of the food is compromised along with our nourishment and digestion. As for cooking purposes, the heat cannot be easily adjusted for accurate cooking temperatures.

Microwave heating uses an electromagnetic microwave generator tuned to a very high frequency, similar to the radiation wave-length (hence, its original name—the radar oven). Heating food in this way has been shown conclusively to destroy from sixty to ninety percent of its vital energy field. Although the minerals in the foods are largely unaffected, the vitamins B-complex, C, and, E, along with other nutritional elements, are significantly decreased. Heating water in a microwave damages the water's magnetic force, a significant factor to consider when heating vegetal foods because they are mostly water.

Bodily effects: Microwave energy is also transformed into heat in the body. Sensitive body parts, such as the eyes, testes, and brain are not able to get rid of the extra heat that builds up over time. A clinical study conducted by Swiss, Russian, and German scientists showed that continually eating microwave food causes long-term permanent brain damage by "shorting out" electrical impulses in the brain (de-polarizing or de-magnetizing the brain tissue). Other studies revealed that both female and male hormone production is severely altered, which can lead to poor egg and sperm health. In addition, substances such as the combination of fat-containing foods and the plastic containers of TV dinners, soups, and instant ramin noodles, for example, release dioxins into the food when they are heated in a microwave. An FDA publication expressed concerned about dioxins resulting from the bleached manufacture of paper goods including milk cartons and some paper containers for microwave dinners. Dioxins are highly toxic carcinogens, which get into the body cells and accumulate, eventually causing abnormal changes in human blood and immune systems.

Even though the microwave's destructive force may not be visible, we can still sense it by the food's weak taste, weak color, and weak aroma. Is the time you may save really worth it?

LAND VEGETABLES

Cleaning Methods

Root Vegetables—(carrots, burdock, daikon radish, etc.): Do not peel because many of their nutrients reside just under skin. Gently scrub the surface with a vegetable brush under cool running water.

Leafy Greens: For larger leaves, hold them by their stems and rinse under cool running water. Clean the crevice well for this is where dirt accumulates. For smaller leaves, fill the sink or a large bowl with cool water and let the leaves soak for about 5 minutes (longer soaking leaches minerals into the water), and then drain and rinse.

Stems: Shear the hard portions of broccoli, cauliflower, kale, etc. off the center stem, and then chop into equal sections.

Cutting Methods

All vegetables can be cut in many ways and each way produces a different energy and therefore a different taste. A meal that combines a variety of shapes is more appealing to the eye and enticing to the taste buds. All cuts should be uniform to ensure even cooking. Knives should be sharpened regularly. Dull blades can easily slip causing injury. Choose a knife you are comfortable using. The most popular types of cuts include:

Diagonal: This exposes more surface area for faster cooking and flavor penetration or simply to provide a more interesting appearance.

Matchstick or julienne: For these cuts, start with the diagonal cut, sliced to the desired thickness. Then neatly stack 3 or 4 slices and slice through lengthwise in 3 or 4 equal cuts.

Half-moon cut: This is used for vegetables such as cucumbers, carrots, parsnips, onions, and broccoli roots. Slice lengthwise, then lay the section on the flat side, and cut across to desired thickness.

Dice and mince: To dice an onion, first cut it in half from root to tip. Place one-half flat side down. Keeping the root end intact, slice vertically from the root end, and then slice horizontally. To dice a root vegetable such as a carrot, cut across into 2-inch lengths or longer. Cut each section in half lengthwise. Place flat side down and slice vertically into 3 or 4 sections, and then horizontally into small cubes. To mince fresh herbs, garlic, etc., finely chop in all directions.

Roll or triangle cut: This is a variation of the diagonal cut. It is used primarily on long and or/fibrous vegetables such as carrot, daikon, parsnip, and asparagus. Slice the vegetable in a diagonal. Roll it a quarter to a third turn away from you and slice straight down. Continue with a diagonal cut and repeat rolling and cutting.

Cooking Methods

Blanch: To lightly cook vegetables and retain their crispness and color, briefly add them to boiling salted water until they wilt, and then immediately remove to a cutting board to stop the cooking process.

Boil: Boiling vegetables for long periods of time destroys most of the plant's nutritional value. Simmer just until tender and then drink the water or use it for soup stock.

Pressure cooking: Place ingredients and water in the pot. Cook on high heat until the pressure comes up. Reduce heat low enough to maintain pressure and cook for required time. When the food is finished cooking, it is best to allow the pressure to come down on its own. Otherwise, place the pot under cool running water until the pressure is released, but do not allow the water to run over the pressure gauge.

Sauté: Start with thinly sliced or small cut vegetables. Preheat the pan over medium to high heat, and then add a small amount of oil to cover the bottom of the pot or skillet. Turn heat to medium low, and if using onions, add the onions first to eliminate the smell. When they turn translucent they are ready. Add white and green vegetables next, followed by orange and yellow. When adding new vegetables, place them in the middle closest to the heat, and oil. Adding a little salt brings out their water. Cover and simmer, adding just enough liquid to prevent scorching. The vegetables should be dry when finished. If not, uncover, turn up the heat, and cook off the water.

Steam: The steamer should sit just above the water line. Add vegetables of the same cut in the steamer. Cook just until tender. For leafy greens, keep the lid slightly ajar to allow air into the pot. This will retain their vibrant color. Save the water for stock or serve as tea. The versatile

Chinese bamboo steamer has multiple, stackable trays that allows you to steam vegetables of different cuts and sizes at the same time, thereby saving time and energy.

Water sauté/oil-water sauté: In a large pot, add about ¼ inch water, a few pinches of sea salt, and minced garlic (optional). Bring to a boil and add finely cut vegetables or chopped leafy greens. Cook, lid slightly opened, for 5 minutes or until vegetables are tender. For oil-water sautéeing, add 1 tablespoon of oil to the water.

Wok stir-frying, Chinese style: In this procedure, the food is always in motion. It cooks quickly over a high heat—thereby retaining its nutrients—with a small amount of oil.

How to season: Heat the wok and add the oil. After a few moments, test the oil with a drop of water. If it sizzles, the wok is hot enough. Add the aromatics such as garlic or ginger. In less than a minute, they will begin to release their flavor and you can begin to add vegetables in the order of their cooking times; those that take the longest go into the wok first. This method keeps the vegetables crisp. Toss the ingredients until they are evenly cooked without scorching. Add the liquid ingredients and seasoning. For thinly sliced or shredded dishes, turn down the heat for a few minutes while the flavors combine, adjust the seasonings, and serve. For dishes with cut ingredients, place a lid over the wok and adjust the temperature to maintain a simmer so that the food steams until it has absorbed a portion or all of the liquid. The basic pattern for many Chinese dishes is to pre-heat the pan or wok, add the oil and heat it, stir-fry the vegetables, add sauce and seasoning, thicken the sauce, and serve.

SEA VEGETABLES (SEAWEEDS)

Preparation

Except for nori sheets, dulse flakes, and agar-agar, briefly rinse the salt off all other sea vegetables under cool water, and then remove any stones or dirt from the crevices. To rehydrate, soak in 3 times water to cover. Because the water contains many of its nutrients, reserve it for cooking or feed it to your plants.

To prepare nori sheets, briefly wave each sheet over a flame until crispy.

For dulse flakes, add directly on foods.

Agar-agar (also called agar) is a variety of red seaweed used as the thickening agent for fruit, custards, puddings, and sauces. It is sold in bar form, flakes, and in powder. I recommend using only the bar and flake forms because the powder has been chemically treated. One bar or 3 to 4 TB of flakes gel 2 cups of liquid.

GRAINS

Basic Cooking Instructions

Rinse—Use a bowl or the cooking pot. Add plenty of cool water and gently rub the grains between the palms of your hands to wash off any dirt or debris. Pour off some of the water to remove any husks that have floated to the top, and then drain the remaining water through a strainer. Repeat this process at least once more or until the water runs clear. For rice, washing off excess starch results in a lighter, fluffier rice.

> **Dash of Wisdom**
>
> With a little experience, you will be able to sense when the grains have finished cooking by sight, sound, and smell: when the water has completely absorbed there is no steam and thus no sight or sound, while the scent of cooked grains is especially aromatic.

Pre-soak—Soaking starts the sprouting process thereby making the grains more digestible. It also reduces cooking time, which saves energy. Soak hard grains in 3 times water to cover overnight at room temperature, or 6 to 8 hours. (Millet and teff berries do not need soaking). Then, discard soaking water.

Fluff—Grains benefit from fluffing. After the steam is released, with a wooden spatula, start by folding the grains from the sides of the pot into the middle; then gently fluff using both the side and flat part of the wooden spatula; and then transfer to a large bowl to cool.

Cooking Methods

Pot cooking: Add the grains and the appropriate amount of fresh water, plus a few pinches of sea salt, and bring to a boil. Cover, reduce heat, and simmer about 1 hour. Do not disturb the cooking process. The momentum of the steam will be lost and the grains will not cook properly.

Pressure cooking: Bring the water, grain, and a few pinches of sea salt up to pressure, then lower the heat and simmer for about 45 minutes.

To avoid burning the grains, use a flame deflector. Turn off the heat and let the pressure come down naturally. Cooked in this way, the grain is very energetic meaning it produces more heat and is therefore more appropriate in cold weather or for frail conditions.

Dry roasting: This is an alternative to the soaking method. Roasting imparts a light texture and nutty taste. Wash and drain the grains, then roast in the cooking pot over medium low heat. Keep them in motion, shaking frequently to avoid burning. While the grains are roasting, boil the appropriate amount of cooking water with a few pinches of sea salt. Add the boiled water to the roasted grains, stir, bring back to a boil, cover, and continue cooking on low heat.

Cooking tips: The grains are finished cooking when they begin to stick to the bottom of the pot; use chopsticks to test as they are gentler than metal. Leftover grain can be prepared as porridge, while leftover porridge can be used to thicken soup or turned into pudding.

Quantities

One cup dry grain serves four. The larger the quantity, the less water is needed.
Pot cooking: A rule of thumb is cups grain cooked in 3¼ water and 3 cups cooked in 4½ cups water.
Pressure cooking: This method requires less water and time than the boiling method. For 2 cups of grain use 1½ cups water; for 3 cups of grain use 4 cups water.

Brown rice varieties: The three types of grain are long, medium, and short. The rule follows that long grain is best in warm weather (cooling effect); short grain is best in cold weather (heat-producing effect); and medium grain is appropriate for all types of weather. Standard ratio given below:

- Short-grain rice has a (sticky) glutinous and chewy texture with a nutty flavor. 1C : 2½C water

- Long-grain rice has a light fluffy texture. 1C : 2C

- Brown rice basmati is a longer grain than long-grain rice and is more aromatic. 1C : 2½C

- Sweet brown is a medium grain with a very glutinous texture. It is best cooked in combination with short or medium grain rice, or with beans. 1C : 2C

Storing

Owing to their natural oils, grains have the potential to become rancid if kept too long at room temperature. Store tightly covered in a cool, dry place for up to 6 months or longer if stored in the refrigerator.

LEGUMES

Except for the short-cooked lentils including yellow lentils (dhal), most all beans contain an enzyme inhibitor and must first be soaked for 12 hours before cooking. Soaking begins the sprouting process, which makes the beans more digestible. Undigested beans can cause gas and a bloated feeling. Cooking dried legumes with a 3-inch strip of kombu seaweed helps speed up the cooking time and greatly increases the nutritional value. Kombu also helps balance the protein and oil in legumes and helps soften their tough fibers, which makes the legumes more digestible. Undercooked beans can cause gas and stomach distress. Beans are thoroughly cooked through when you can mash them with a fork. Reasons why some people experience problems with flatulence and allergies can be due to poor food combining, improper food preparation, lack of digestive enzymes, and/ or wrong choice of legume. Lentils and the smaller beans, aduki, and peas are the easiest to digest.*

Approximate simmering times: Kidney bean, chickpeas (garbanzo), white beans—1½ to 2 hours pot cooking or 45 minutes pressure cooking; black beans—2½ hours pot cooking or 1¼ hours pressure cooking; mung beans, lentils, and split green peas—1 hour pot cooking or 30 to 40 minutes pressure cooking; aduki beans—1½ hours pot cooking or 30 to 45 minutes pressure cooking.*

Preparing dried beans and peas

Sort and rinse—On a clean kitchen towel or table, sort out any shriveled beans or peas, pebbles, and insects and then rinse in cool water.

Long soak method—Add water about 3 inches above the beans, or 4 to 5 cups water per cup beans. Soak at room temperature or, in warm weather, soak in the fridge to avoid fermentation. Drain and discard soaking water. Rinse in cool water and proceed with cooking.

Short soak/boil method—If long soaking is not possible, this method can be used effectively. Boil beans in 3 times water to cover for 3 minutes in a heavy-bottomed pot. Cover and set aside for 2 to 4 hours (longer soaking does not help or hurt). Then follow the simmering times above. This method can reduce hard-to-digest complex sugars by 80 percent.

Cooking instructions

Each cup of dried beans and peas yields 2 to 2 ½ cups cooked. Cook in a large, covered pot, preferably a pressure cooker. The exceptions are baby lima beans and red beans, both of which create foam that can clog the pressure gauge.

1. Rinse the salt off a 3-inch strip of kombu seaweed. Place on the bottom of the cooking pot; add the beans, then the water. For soup, use 3 to 4 cups water for each cup of dry legumes, or at least 1 inch above the top of the beans for bean dishes.

2. Bring to a boil and remove any foam that rises to the top. Add the vegetables, and any of the following digestive herbs and spices: ginger and/or garlic cloves; the spices turmeric, coriander, and cumin. Cover and simmer.

3. You can include any leafy green spices such as oregano, basil, and thyme 30 to 45 minutes before beans are due to be done. Spicing too early can cause the flavors to break down.

4. Salt or salted products, or sweet and other acidic foods such as tomatoes or vinegar can be added when the legumes are 80 percent cooked. Both salt and acid/sweet foods will toughen uncooked beans and considerably slow down the cooking process.

5. Allow flavors to blend for at least 30 minutes before serving.

6. Add lemon or lime juice directly to the pot after cooking or in individual serving bowls.

7. Umeboshi vinegar combines well with bean dishes. Add a dash or two in each serving bowl.

Quantities

1 lb. serves 6 to 8.

Storing

Store in an airtight glass jar away from heat. Use within 6 months. Cooked beans freeze very well.

TIPS OF THE TRADE

- Recipes are not set in stone. Use your intuition.

- Rotate your foods. Eating the same foods over and over again leads to narrow-minded thinking.

- Foods that grow together go together.

- Eat the whole food for perfect balance. This means eating vegetables such as radish, celery, carrot, or fennel along with their leaves and fronds.

- It is best to cook only the amount of food you will consume during the day it is cooked, or at most, the following day. Refrigeration and time reduce their life energy.

- Avoid eating too many acidic nightshade vegetables—ones that grow at night: tomato, eggplant, bell peppers, summer squash, white potato, huckleberry, and hot pepper. This also includes prepared foods made with nightshades such as ketchup, paprika, Tabasco, and chili powder.

- Over-cooked and over-boiled vegetables lose their nutrient value and are hard to digest.

- When steaming or boiling vegetables, some nutrients leach into the water. Use it for soup stock or as tea.

- Tear lettuce, rather than cutting it, to prevent the edges from browning.

- To extract any bitterness from a cucumber, cut a one-third inch slice off one end of the cucumber and rub both ends together in a fast circular motion. Wash off any foam that rises to the surface and re-peat with the other side.

- Liquids and foods should not be taken when they are too hot or too cold. Hot debilitates; cold paralyzes.

- Hot spices and hot peppers cool the body.

- Add fresh herbs near the end of the cooking process to prevent them from becoming bitter.

- A wooden cutting board is safer and more hygienic than synthetic. Wood holds the edge of the blade so it does not slip; the small grooves caused by knife strokes trap and smother bacteria inside the wood, while synthetic boards tend to breed bacteria. Dry a wood cutting board in the sun to sterilize it.

- Use natural light to work in whenever possible. Avoid eco bulbs (as well as other neon lighting). Not only do eco bulbs give off nega-tive energy; researchers claim they can release potentially harmful amounts of mercury if broken. Levels of toxic vapor around smashed eco-bulbs were up to 20 times higher than the safe guideline limit for an indoor area, the study said. It added that broken bulbs posed a potential health risk to pregnant women, babies, and small children.

- Work in fresh circulating air as opposed to air conditioning and forced heat. However, if you work in a closed environment or live under heavily polluted skies, consider an air purifier that generates ion ozone emissions. This will also help eliminate mold and bacteria.

- Get acquainted with your food. As you wash and cut up the vegeta-bles, appreciate their bumpy, sleek, or fuzzy textures and wonderful aromas.

- Keep your working space free from clutter. Disorder and chaos in the kitchen will ultimately be reflected in your food.

- Cleanliness is next to Godliness.

- Attitude is everything. When preparing your food, eliminate nega-tive distractions for your kitchen is a sacred place.

Food is our highest medicine

PART 5 ~ THE RECIPES

"Our lives are not in the lap of the gods,
but in the lap of our cooks."
—Lin Yutang—

Food is our highest medicine

BREAKFAST

A breakfast of unrefined whole grains provides long lasting energy and alertness.

WHOLE GRAIN PORRIDGES

For more nutrition, blend 2 TB freshly ground golden flax seeds in each serving bowl.

Flax seed is high in omega-3 essential fatty acid (EFA), which is vital for strengthening immunity and cleansing the heart and arteries. It is also high in fiber and mucilage, which acts as a natural laxative and thus benefits the colon. Because the seeds expand 20 times in volume, a generous amount of water or other liquid should be taken along with the seeds. In their whole form, the seeds are hard to digest and therefore must be ground before consuming. Since nutrient value begins to degrade shortly after grinding, consume immediately. (Purchase only whole flax seeds.) Although both golden and brown seeds have the same nutritional value, the golden variety has a more delicate texture and thus grinds to a finer consistency.

BROWN RICE AND SWEET BROWN RICE

Serves 4 or more.

Soak equal amounts of both grains overnight. The ratio for rice porridge is commonly 1 cup rice to 5 cups water. Use more or less water depending on the consistency you prefer. Add ¼ tsp. sea salt to the cooking water. Simmer 2 hours in a pot or 1 hour in a pressure cooker.

Cooking tip: For variety, combine 70 percent brown rice with 30 percent other grain such as rye, whole barley, wild rice, or wheatberries, which add a nutty texture; other combinations are millet, oats, groats, and corn.

MILLET

Serves 4

½ cup millet, soaked

Few pinches sea salt

Use 6 cups water for pot cooking; 4 cups for pressure cooking. Simmer 1 hour or more in a pot, or 40 minutes in a pressure cooker.

OAT GROUTS

Serves around 4

1 cup oat grouts, soaked overnight

3 cups water for pot cooking

2 cups water for pressure cooking

Cinnamon to taste

Add oats to water and simmer 1½ to 2 hours in a pressure cooker or 40 minutes in a in a pot. Sprinkle cinnamon on top of each serving bowl.

Dash of Wisdom

Oat grouts are sweet and chewy and have the highest nutritional value of all forms of oats. They also digest slowly, which reduces the glycemic load and also makes them quite filling.

PERUVIAN

Serves 4

½ cup amaranth
½ cup quinoa
2 cups water
Few pinches sea salt

Thoroughly rinse quinoa and amaranth in a fine mesh strainer. Simmer all ingredients for about 20 minutes.

POLENTA

Serves 4

½ cup stone ground corn meal
3 cups water
¼ tsp. sea salt

Add all ingredients to a large pot and bring to a boil, stirring frequently to prevent lumping. Simmer for about 30 to 35 minutes. Polenta thickens as it cooks, so you may need to add more boiling water to maintain a fairly soft consistency. The porridge is finished cooking when the mixture easily comes away from the sides of the pot.

Cooking tip: Serve as a light evening meal accompanied by a dish with a contrasting, crunchy texture such as a salad or lightly sautéed onions and carrots.

ROASTED RYE FLAKES

Serves 2 to 4

1 cup rye flakes
3 or 4 cups boiling water
Few pinches sea salt

Dry roast the rye flakes in the cooking pot. Add the boiling water and sea salt, cover, and simmer until soft.

TEFF BERRY

Serves 4

Teff has a creamy and sticky texture with a molasses flavor from naturally occurring yeast that ferments when moist. Roasting adds a rich flavor and a crunchy texture.

1 cup teff berries
4 cups boiling water
¼ tsp.sea salt

Dry roast the teff berries in the cooking pot. Add the boiling water and sea salt, cover, and simmer for about 40 minutes.

TRADITIONAL CORN BREAD
Serves 6–8
4 cups water
1 cup stone ground corn meal
¼ tsp. sea salt
Sprigs of rosemary (optional)
Corn or olive oil
Preheat oven to 325°F.
In a large pot, bring water, corn meal and sea salt to a slow boil, stirring frequently to avoid lumping.
Add the rosemary and simmer for 15 minutes.
Lightly oil a glass or ceramic baking dish, fill with the corn mixture, and add a little oil on top.
Bake for 30 to 40 minutes or until golden brown.

MOCHI AND MOCHI WAFFLES
1 package any variety of brown rice mochi
Sesame oil
Slice mochi into 2-inch squares.
Stove-top method: Coat a cast iron or other heavy skillet with sesame oil and heat. Add the mochi squares. Mochi expands when cooked, so allow space between each square. Cover and cook on medium low heat until the bottoms have browned. Then repeat with the other side and cook until the mochi squares puff up.
Oven method: Bake in a preheated 300°F oven or toaster oven.

Mochi waffles—Slice mochi package into fourths. Lightly oil a waffle maker, add mochi, and heat until brown.

CORN, APPLE, AND SUNFLOWER SEED MUFFINS
Yields 12 muffins
Dry ingredients
2 cups whole wheat flour
1 cup cornmeal
1 TB non-aluminum baking powder
1 tsp. cinnamon
Handful sunflower seeds
¼ tsp. sea salt
Wet ingredients
2 apples, any variety
½ cup coconut or light sesame oil
¾–1 cup hemp seed milk (pg. 136) or other unsweetened vegan milk

4 oz. silken or soft tofu

Sweetening choices

½ cup syrup of choice or several drops stevia dark concentrate combined with the wet ingredients or 1 TB dried stevia leaves or powder combined with the dry ingredients

Preheat oven to 350°F.

Mix dry ingredients together in a large bowl.

Grate the apples and blend together with the rest of the wet ingredients.

Add the wet ingredients to the dry ingredients and stir gently to mix evenly—do not over mix.

Oil a 12-serving muffin tin. Fill each section to the top and sprinkle sunflower seeds on top.

Bake 40 to 50 minutes or until the top is golden brown and a toothpick comes out clean when inserted into the center of a muffin.

BANANA PANCAKES

Serves 4 to 6

Wet ingredients

1½ cups coconut water, unsweetened soymilk, or hemp seed milk (pg. 136)

2 bananas, mashed

1 TB pure vanilla extract

1 TB coconut or red palm oil

Dry ingredients

2 TB freshly ground golden flax seeds

¾ cup oat flour—blend rolled oats in a coffee grinder

¾ cup stone ground, whole wheat flour

½ tsp. cinnamon

In a bowl, stir together the ground flax seeds with coconut water or vegan milk.

Wait a few minutes until the seeds have absorbed the liquid, and then blend in the rest of the wet ingredients.

In a separate bowl, mix together the dry ingredients.

Add the dry ingredients to the wet ingredients and stir gently to blend.

In a skillet, heat oil to very hot, but not to the smoking point.

Use a ladle to measure each pancake.

Fry until the bottom is golden brown. Flip and repeat with the other side.

Serving suggestion: As a topping for the pancakes, simmer any fruit of the season in a little water with a pinch of sea salt and your choice of spices. Purée if desired.

Cooking tip: Ground flax seeds serve as an egg replacement.

LAND VEGETABLES

Dark leafy green vegetables—kale, collards, mustard, dandelion, bok choy, spinach, Swiss chard, watercress, arugula, leafy lettuce, and fresh herbs—are excellent sources of chlorophyll and vitamins D and A. Chlorophyll is needed to build blood, and clean blood purifies the liver; vitamin D is necessary for the production of insulin; and vitamin A (beta-carotene) plays many key roles in the metabolic processes of the liver. Research has shown that when greens and other beta-carotene foods (orange-red) such as carrots are consumed in more than average amounts, the incidence of cancer of the lungs, stomach, colon, bladder, uterus, ovaries, and skin are considerably reduced.

SOUPS

Serve soup comfortably warm so that the delicate flavors can be appreciated. Above all, if soup is taken too hot, it may burn the tongue and intestines.

For flavoring with miso, refer to page 47 for instructions.

VEGETABLE STOCK

The secret to a good soup is in the stock. Keep in mind that root vegetables produce a sweeter taste.

7 cups water
6 dried shitake mushrooms
3-inch strip kombu
2 carrots including tops, chopped
1 parsnip, chopped
1 rutabaga, chopped
2 onions, chopped
2 stalks celery and leaves, chopped
½ tsp. sea salt
Other suggestions: celery root, fennel bulb, parsley root, turnip

Rinse shitakes and soak in very hot water to cover until soft.
Soak kombu in water to cover for 15 minutes.
Gently scrub the root vegetables.
In a large pot, bring all ingredients including shitake and kombu soaking waters to a boil, cover and simmer 1 hour, or longer if you prefer a more hearty broth. Strain to remove vegetables.

Dash of Wisdom

The combination of these plant foods provides a wealth of minerals as well as vitamins A, B, and C.

MISO SOUP

Serves 3 to 4

This soup provides long lasting energy. In Japan, it is traditionally served for breakfast.

4 cups water or vegetable stock
4 large dried shitake mushrooms
2 strips dried wakame
¼ lb. firm or soft tofu
1 onion cut in half moons
1 carrot cut in half moons
2 TB finely grated ginger root
2 scant TB brown rice or chickpea miso
2 scallions finely slivered

Dash of Wisdom

In the Orient, shitake is used in the treatment of cancer, especially cancers of the stomach and cervix.* In the West, research shows shitake supports the immune and cardiovascular systems.

Rinse shitakes and soak in very hot water to cover until soft. Drain and reserve the soaking water. Remove the stems with a scissors and discard, and then cut into thin slices. Rinse wakame, and soak in enough water to cover for a few minutes.

Slice tofu into bite-size cubes.

In a pot, add vegetable stock or water, shitake and wakame along with their soaking waters, tofu, vegetables, and ginger.

Simmer about 20 minutes or until the vegetables are soft.

Add diluted miso and gently simmer for a few minutes.

Garnish each bowl with scallions.

Cooking tip: Instead of a carrot, try other root vegetables such as daikon radish, parsnip, turnip, or a combination.

CLEAR GINGER AND NOODLES
Serves 4

2 pre-bundled or 2 handfuls soba or udon noodles
4 cups vegetable stock
2 TB finely grated ginger root
2 TB shoyu
Several scallions finely slivered

Dash of Wisdom

Ginger alleviates high blood pressure; it stimulates circulation and relaxes the muscles surrounding blood vessels, which facilitates blood flow throughout the body.

Cook noodles according to package instructions. Drain, rinse, and place in individual soup bowls.

Heat the stock, add the ginger and shoyu and simmer for several minutes. Pour over the noodles and garnish with the scallions.

CREAMY WINTER SQUASH AND MOCHI CROUTONS
Serves 4 or more

The creamy texture of this soup has a nurturing effect. Its exotic taste is due primarily to the curry's blend of spices that usually includes cumin, fenugreek, turmeric, and coriander.

Dash of Wisdom

Winter squash nurtures the pancreas and spleen*; the curry spices, along with cinnamon, are effective in controlling blood sugar and cholesterol levels.

½ package any variety of mochi
4 cups stock or water
1 butternut or buttercup squash
1 large onion, diced
1 chunk ginger root
1 TB stevia dried leaf
¼ tsp. cinnamon
1 tsp. curry
2 TB brown rice or chickpea miso

Preheat oven to 300°F.

Do not peel the squash, just gently scrub the surface. Then cut in half, remove the seeds, and chop.

In a large pot, add the stock or water, vegetables, herb, and spices. Simmer for 30 minutes or until the squash is soft. Remove the ginger and discard.

Dilute miso with some soup broth, add back to the pot and gently simmer for a few minutes.

While the soup is cooking, cut mochi into bite-size pieces. Place on an oiled baking sheet, leaving space between each mochi to expand, and bake until they puff up, around 5 minutes.

Purée the soup in batches. Top each serving bowl with mochi squares.

Cooking tip: When choosing a squash, look for one that feels heavy for its size. For buttercup squash, choose one with raised nodules on the skin and a deep orange color pulp. These are good indications that the squash is fully ripe and sweet.

CORN CHOWDER
Serves 6

6 ears of corn or 2 cups kernels

5 cups stock or water

1 TB olive or light sesame oil

1 onion, diced

Sea salt

1 yam or sweet potato

½ cup oat flour, or flakes ground in a coffee mill

1 cup loosely packed dulse

1–2 tsp. stevia dried leaf

2 TB chickpea or other light colored miso

Dash of Wisdom

Corn helps overcome sexual weakness.*

Cut the corn off the cob.

Gently scrub yam/sweet potato and cut into small cubes.

Heat oil in a soup pot, then add onions and a few pinches sea salt and sauté for 1 minute. Mix in the sweet potatoes and corn.

Add the water/stock, oat flour, dulse, and stevia and simmer for 30 minutes. Dilute the miso, add back to the pot, and gently simmer for a few minutes.

PUREÉD SWEET POTATO AND LEEK
Serves 4

4 cups stock or water

2 sweet potatoes

2 leeks chopped

1 stalk celery including leaves

Chunk ginger root

1 TB dried stevia leaf

¼ tsp. sea salt

Several sprigs of cilantro

Gently scrub the potato skin and cut into bite-size cubes. Simmer all ingredients until the sweet potatoes are cooked through.

Remove and discard the ginger root and the celery and its leaves.

Purée the soup in batches.

Garnish each serving bowl with cilantro.

Dash of Wisdom

Sweet potato nurtures the pancreas and spleen and, because it is high in vitamin A, it improves eyesight; the leek's sour and pungent flavor benefits the liver.*

BEET BORSCHT AND TOFU DILL SOUR CREAM

Serves 3 or 4

2 lbs. beets

Sea salt

Dash of Wisdom

Beets cleanse the blood, which improves circulation.*

Sour cream

6 oz. soft or silken tofu

2 TB brown rice or apple cider vinegar

1 TB lemon juice or umeboshi vinegar

1 tsp. rice syrup, or to taste

Garnish

¼ cup diced cucumbers

¼ cup diced sweet onions

Handful minced dill

Wash and cut beets into quarters, then steam until soft. Reserve the water. Remove the skins when cooled.

In a blender, purée beets with its cooking water and a few pinches sea salt. Cool in the refrigerator.

Rinse out the blender and add the sour cream ingredients and just enough water, if necessary, to blend.

To serve, place diced cucumbers and onions on the bottom of each serving bowl, add the beet soup, and top with minced dill.

COOL CUCUMBER MINT

Serves 2

6 oz. silken or soft tofu

½ cup fresh mint leaves

½ cup sweet onion, chopped

2 medium cucumbers, chopped

2 TB fresh dill, chopped

⅓ cup lemon juice

1 TB sweet white miso

1 tsp. finely ground stevia leaf
Hungarian paprika
Handful mint leaves, minced

Steam tofu for 5 minutes; uncover and cool. Mince half the mint leaves and set aside for garnish. Purée tofu with other ingredients. Garnish each bowl with a sprinkle of paprika and minced mint on top. Serve chilled.

SAVORY DISHES

LEAFY GREENS AND SHALLOTS

Serves 4

Other dark leafy greens can be substituted for collards such as kale, mustard, dandelion, spinach, or Swiss chard.

¾ lb. collard greens
1 TB olive oil for sautéing
2 shallots, chopped
Sea salt

Remove the stems of the collards and trim.
Steam the leaves and stems until the leaves are tender, but still vibrant green. Remove immediately to a cutting board.
Chop the stems, then stack the leaves and slice vertically and then horizontally into equal sections.
Sauté the shallots with a few pinches sea salt until shallots turn translucent. Turn off the heat and blend in the greens and stems. Add a bit more oil if desired.

WILD GREENS

Many wild green leafy plants are edible. Two of my favorites are dandelion and stinging nettles. Pick them early in the morning when the dew still clings to their leaves. (Use gloves for the nettles.) Gather plants that grow in a pristine environment, and not by the side of a road.

Stinging nettle—The leaves become sweet and tender when cooked. To prepare, blanch briefly until they wilt, then remove immediately.
Dandelion—To prepare, remove the flower and discard. Remove the root, wash well, and save for soup stock. Add the leaves to soup at

the end of the cooking process, or heat a small amount of oil and sauté leaves briefly with a pinch of sea salt.

The leaves can also be served raw—chop and add to cooked salads such as potato or noodle.

CHINESE CABBAGE AND CARAWAY WITH UMEBOSHI SAUCE

Serves 4

1 medium Chinese cabbage

1 TB sesame oil

2 scallions

Umeboshi sauce

Blend together:

2 TB arrowroot or kuzu dissolved in 1 cup room temperature water

2 tsp. umeboshi paste or 2 minced umeboshi plums

2 TB mirin

¼ cup roasted caraway seeds (pg. 131)

Dash of Wisdom

Caraway seeds counteract the cabbage's gas-forming tendencies; chewing your food very well will also minimize gas.*

Rinse the cabbage and discard any discolored leaves. Separate the leaves, transfer to a cutting board, and stack. Either cut the leaves into ½-inch strips or 1-inch squares.

Slice the scallions in half lengthwise, and then slice each section into thin strips.

In a large pot, add about an inch of water, oil, and cabbage and sauté until tender.

Add the scallions, then blend in the umeboshi sauce and simmer a few minutes stirring constantly until it thickens. Then blend in the caraway seeds.

FENNEL AND LACINTO KALE WITH FENNEL FROND DRESSING

Serves 4

2 fennel bulbs with fronds

¾ lb. lacinto kale

3 TB roasted fennel seeds (pg. 131)

Dash of Wisdom

In small amounts, the mildly pungent flavor of fennel stimulates a sluggish liver; it also moves energy through the body and speeds up metabolism, which aids in weight loss.*

Steam the fennel bulbs until just barely tender. Remove to a cutting board and cut into quarters.

Wash the kale, remove and discard the tips of the stems, and steam until tender, but still vibrant green. Remove to a cutting board, stack and cut into equal bite size squares.

Fennel frond dressing

Minced fennel fronds

2–4 garlic cloves, minced

Pinch sea salt

¼ cup olive oil

Blend all ingredients together in a small bowl. For best results, use a mortar and pestle.

In a bowl, blend the kale with fennel frond dressing.

To serve: Place the seasoned kale in the center of a serving plate, arrange the fennel bulbs around it, and garnish with roasted fennel seeds.

SAUTÉED MEMBERS OF THE ONION FAMILY

Serves 4

2 onions
Few pinches sea salt
4 or 5 garlic cloves, minced
1 leek
3 or 4 scallions
Handful chives
2 TB sesame oil
2 TB mirin
1 TB tamari

Dash of Wisdom

All members of the onion family lower cholesterol and blood sugar; promote warmth and thus move energy through the body, which helps reduce clotting.*

Slice onions into 4 or 5 sections from top to bottom keeping each section intact by its stem. Then gently fan.

Carefully clean the crevices of the leek and remove the stem and tip. Separate the white part from the green. Slice the white part in half, and then slice vertically into thin strips. Slice the green part into diagonals. Chop the scallions and chives.

Heat the oil in a wok or large fry pan. Add the onions and a few pinches sea salt and sauté briefly. Stir in the garlic, then the leek, and then add the mirin and tamari, cover, and simmer until leeks are soft.

Blend in the scallions and chives and cook briefly until they wilt.

Serve small amounts.

CARROTS, LEEKS, AND GARLIC IN GINGER KUZU SAUCE

Serves 4

2 carrots, thinly sliced on the diagonal
1 large leek, sliced diagonally
1 TB sesame oil
Several garlic cloves, cut into slivers
Few pinches sea salt

Ginger kuzu sauce

2 TB finely grated ginger root
2 TB kuzu
1 cup stevia marinade (pg. 135)

Dash of Wisdom

Carrots strengthen the pancreas and spleen, improve the function of the liver, and dissolve stones and tumors; leek's pungent and sour flavor is astringent, which benefits the liver; garlic promotes circulation.*

In a wok or fry pan, heat the oil, add the garlic, and a few pinches sea salt and stir-fry briefly.

Add the carrots and stir-fry for a couple of minutes.

Add the leeks and around a third cup of water, cover, and simmer until carrots are soft.

Stir the sauce again, then add to the carrots and leeks, and stir until the sauce thickens. Remove from the heat and serve.

OIL-WATER SAUTÉED CABBAGE AND ONION

Serves 4

1 TB sesame oil

1 small head cabbage washed, cored, and quartered

2 onions, quartered and separated

1 tsp. fennel seeds

Sea salt

Umeboshi vinegar

Ground black peppercorns to taste

Dash of Wisdom

Cabbage purifies the blood and destroys parasites; its dark, outer leaves are high in vitamin E and contain 1/3 more calcium than inner leaves; fennel helps counteract cabbage's gas-forming tendencies; pepper stimulates energy flow in the body.

In a large pot, add about ½-inch water, oil, cabbage, onions, fennel seeds, and a few pinches sea salt.

Bring to a boil, cover, and simmer until cabbage is soft.

Remove to a serving bowl, add a splash of umeboshi vinegar, and sprinkle with pepper.

OIL-WATER SAUTÉED CAULIFLOWER AND BROCCOLI

Serves 4

1 head cauliflower

1 head broccoli

Several garlic cloves, chopped

1 TB sesame or coconut oil

Sea salt

Few TB roasted cumin seeds (pg. 131)

Dash of Wisdom

Broccoli and cauliflower are recommended by the National Cancer Institute for cancer prevention.

Remove the flowerets from the cauliflower and separate.

Remove the broccoli stem, then trim and chop.

Remove the broccoli leaves and save; separate the flowerets.

In a wide pot, add about a half cup of water, oil, and salt and bring to a boil. Add the cauliflower and broccoli, cover, and cook on medium-high heat until the vegetables are still vibrant green and crisp-tender.

Remove immediately to a serving bowl and sprinkle on roasted seeds.

CREAMY SUNCHOKES

Serves 4

The sunchoke, also called Jerusalem artichoke, is a sweet tuber native to North America and a relative of the sunflower. This dish will remind you of mashed potatoes.

1 lb. sunchokes

¼ tsp. sea salt

Gently scrub the sunchokes, and then slice evenly. Steam just until soft. Save some of the cooking water for blending.

In a blender or food processor, add the sunchokes, sea salt, and just enough cooking water to blend until smooth.

Cooking tip: Sunchokes can also be enjoyed raw.

Dash of Wisdom

Sunchoke contains inulin, a natural fructose, which is known to stimulate insulin production and to lower blood sugar levels.

ASPARAGUS WITH LEMON DRESSING

Serves 4 to 6

2 handfuls asparagus

Lemon dressing

Equal amounts lemon juice and oil of choice

Few pinches sea salt

Cut off the woody portion of the stem, and then slice the remaining stem into diagonals.

Steam the stems for a few minutes, then add the asparagus, and steam until soft, but still crisp and vibrant green.

Arrange on a platter and drizzle on the dressing.

Dash of Wisdom

Asparagus helps cleanse the arteries of cholesterol while its diuretic properties benefit the kidneys; however, too much asparagus can irritate the kidneys.*

BURDOCK AND OTHER ROOTS

Serves 4

The skin of burdock root contains its nutrients and earthy flavor. Burdock can be steamed, stir-fried, or added to soups and stews. While slicing the burdock, drop slices in water with a little lemon juice or vinegar to prevent discoloration. Drain before cooking. Burdock root can be stored for up to a week in the refrigerator or kept in cold storage for 2 to 6 months.

2 TB sesame oil

1 onion, cut in half moons

Sea salt

1 carrot, cut into matchsticks

1 parsnip, peeled and cut into matchsticks

1 cup stevia ginger lemonade or stevia marinade (pg. 135)

Tamari

Dash of Wisdom

Burdock, known as gobo in Japan, is a mildly bitter herb that significantly purifies the blood, reduces fat, and regulates blood sugar.

2 scallions, sliced diagonally

¼ cup roasted sesame seeds (pg. 131)

Trim the ends of the burdock root, then gently scrub and cut into slivers. Heat oil in a large, heavy skillet or wok. Add the onions and a few pinches sea salt and sauté for 30 seconds.

Add the burdock root, carrots and parsnips and sauté for 2 minutes, stirring frequently.

Add about a half-cup stevia, a few dashes tamari, cover, and cook on medium high heat for several minutes. Add enough stevia liquid to prevent burning.

Add the scallions, turn up the heat, and cook until the liquid has evaporated. Transfer to a serving bowl and blend in the sesame seeds.

STIR-FRIED BABY BOK CHOY AND GARLIC CHIVES

Serves 4

Baby bok choy is smaller and sweeter than the larger variety. The garlic chive is the top of the garlic plant. It has a distinct garlic flavor and its shape is similar to a slender leek.

Several baby bok choy

Handful garlic chives, chopped

1 TB sesame oil

Tamari

Dash of Wisdom

According to the Law of Similarities, bok choy looks like bone and contains the same 23% amount of sodium as bone, and thus specifically targets bone strength. Without enough sodium in the diet, the body pulls it from the bones, making them weak.

Trim the bok choy, rinse any dirt from the crevices, and then shake off excess water.

Heat the oil and add the bok choy. Toss to evenly coat, add a few splashes of tamari, lower heat, cover, and cook until the stems have softened adding just enough water to prevent burning.

Toss in the garlic chives and sauté until wilted.

Serve immediately.

Cooking tip: This dish combines well with Sweet and spicy tofu triangles (pg. 116).

STIR-FRIED BITTER MELON

Serves 4

Bitter melon looks somewhat like a large cucumber, and is among the most bitter tasting vegetables. Combining it with a sweet flavor will offset the bitter taste while garlic or chili pepper will mask it. When first picked, it is yellow-green, but as it ripens, it turns to a

Dash of Wisdom

Bitter melon has been shown to lower blood sugar levels and has been used for centuries in Asia, east Africa, and parts of the Amazon to treat diabetes.

yellow-orange color. Choose melons that are still green for a more bitter flavor and a yellow-orange melon for a milder taste. Select firm, unblemished melons that are from 5 to 12 inches in length. They are available fresh from April to September in Asian markets and in some health food stores.

2 TB tamari

3 drops stevia dark concentrate

2 TB lemon juice

1 lb. bitter melon

1 TB minced garlic

½ tsp. chili pepper flakes

Pinch sea salt

2 TB red palm, coconut, or sesame oil

In a cup, combine tamari, stevia, and lemon juice.

Cut bitter melon in half lengthwise and discard the seeds and fibrous core. (The skin contains its valuable nutrients.)

To reduce bitterness, either blanch the melon in boiling water for 2 to 3 minutes or, more effective, roll the sliced pieces in salt, leave for 30 minutes, then squeeze out the juice, and then rinse and dry.

In a small bowl, mash the chili pepper flakes with the minced garlic and blend in the sea salt.

Heat the oil, add garlic/chili mixture ,and stir-fry briefly until aromatic. Add the bitter melon and stir-fry for about 2 minutes, and then add the tamari/lemon/stevia mixture.

Cook for another 1 to 2 minutes, until the bitter melon browns and begins to soften.

PARSLEY POTATO SALAD WITH LEMON VINAIGRETTE

Serves 4

Several small Yukon gold potatoes

1 purple onion, cut into half moons

1 cup parsley, finely chopped

Whole black peppercorns to taste

Lemon vinaigrette

Equal amounts lemon juice and oil (olive, sacha inchi, or argan)

1 scant tsp. syrup of choice (pg. 56)

Sea salt to taste

Dash of Wisdom

Potato neutralizes body acids, which helps relieve arthritis and rheumatism; its high potassium content balances high salt and sodium diets, including meat; if eaten with its skin, the potato is considered one of the most completely nourishing foods.*

Wash and cut potatoes into quarters. Steam until soft, then transfer to a large bowl to cool.

Mix in the onions, parsley, and ground pepper, and then blend in the dressing and whole peppercorns.

Allow flavors to blend for at least one hour before serving.

Caution: Green potatoes and sprouts that grow on potatoes are toxic—be sure to remove the eye of the sprout imbedded in the potato.*

COBB SALAD (VEGETARIAN STYLE)

Serves 4 or more

A Cobb salad consists of various finely cut lettuces and other raw and cooked vegetables.

Sweet and spicy tofu triangles (pg. 116)

1 head cauliflower

½ cup red leaf lettuce

½ cup arugula

½ cup endive

2 cups cherry tomatoes, quartered

1 sweet or Vidalia onion, diced

5 large black olives, rinsed

Vinaigrette

3 TB olive oil

3 TB vinegar of choice

2 TB finely grated ginger root

3 drops stevia dark concentrate

Sea salt or shoyu to taste

Dash of Wisdom

The bitter flavor of arugula, endive and olive benefit the liver; tomato relieves high blood pressure and other symptoms of a stressed liver such as headache and red eyes.*

Cut seasoned tofu into bite-size pieces.

Steam only the cauliflowerets and separate.

Rinse, dry, and finely chop all lettuces. Pit and slice the olives.

In a large bowl, toss the cauliflower, lettuces, tomato, and onions with the dressing. Then blend in the tofu and olives.

TARTY STEAMED BEETS

Serves 4

1 small bunch of beets

1 tsp. umeboshi vinegar

Handful minced cilantro, parsley, or dill

Dash of Wisdom

Beet strengthens the heart and benefits the liver.*

Wash and quarter beets.

Steam either in a pressure cooker for 15 minutes or a pot for around 30 minutes, until a fork easily pierces the skin. Remove to a cutting board and let cool, and then remove the skins and cut beets into slices. Drizzle on the umeboshi vinegar and sprinkle with choice of garnish.

RAW SALADS

Raw vegetables, sprouts, and fruits are high in enzymes, which stimulates energy flow.

For a truly raw effect, use stone pressed olive oil, unroasted argan or sacha inchi oil, or cold pressed hemp, chia, or flax oil.

MINTY CARROT, KOHLRABI, AND TURNIP SLAW WITH CINNAMON DRESSING
Serves 4

1 carrot with leaves
1 kohlrabi, peeled
1 turnip, peeled
1 cup mint leaves, minced
Several red radishes, diced

Cinnamon dressing
3 TB oil of choice
3 TB lemon juice
Pinch sea salt or dash of shoyu
½ tsp. cinnamon
3 drops stevia dark concentrate

Dash of Wisdom

Kohlrabi and turnip treat blood sugar imbalance; carrot leaves are rich in vitamin A; radish removes deposits and stones from the gallbladder; mint cleanses heart and arteries.*

Grate equal amounts of turnip, kohlrabi, and carrot. Chop the carrot leaves. Toss all ingredients together in a large bowl and gently fold in the vinaigrette. Place a small mound of slaw on each serving plate.

CUCUMBER STUFFED WITH FENUGREEK SALSA
Serves 4

2 small cucumbers cut in half-lengthwise. Scoop out the seeds and save.

Fenugreek salsa
Juice of 2 limes
1 TB roasted fenugreek seeds (pg. 131)
1 tsp. minced ginger
2 garlic cloves, minced
½ tsp. ground coriander
1 or 2 drops stevia dark concentrate
2 green chilies, minced (remove seeds for milder flavor)
Cucumber seeds
Pinch sea salt

Dash of Wisdom

Cucumber lifts depression; coriander helps relieve anxiety; and fenugreek reduces blood sugar and cholesterol levels.*

Use a mortar and pestle for best results. Crush the first 5 salsa ingredients, then blend in the remaining ingredients.

Fill each cucumber half with the mixture.

AVOCADO, ARUGULA, FENNEL, AND WALNUT
Serves 4

2 cups arugula, chopped

1 fennel bulb with fronds

1 Hass avocado, sliced in half moons

½ cup roasted walnuts, chopped (pg. 131)

Dressing

1/3 cup olive oil (or oil of choice)

¼ cup lemon juice

3 drops stevia dark concentrate

Few pinches course sea salt

Dash of Wisdom

Avocado is high in protein and fat. The fat is easily digested and will not distress the liver if consumed in small amounts; walnut benefits the kidney and nourishes the brain*; arugula is high in chlorophyll which is healing to the liver.

Chop the arugula and place in a large bowl.

Slice the fennel bulb into strips and mince the fronds. Mix together with the arugula.

Place arugula and fennel in the center of a serving plate and arrange the avocado slices around it.

Drizzle on the dressing and sprinkle with walnuts.

MESCLUN GREENS AND TANGERINES
Serves 2 to 4

Salad ingredients

2 loosely packed cups mesclun greens

Several red radishes, thinly sliced

1 tangerine; separate the sections

½ cup roasted sunflower seeds (pg. 131)

Dressing (blend separately)

3 TB oil of choice

3 TB lemon juice

2 or 3 drops stevia dark concentrate

Sea salt

Dash cayenne pepper

Dash of Wisdom

Radish detoxifies; tangerines balance highly acidic conditions such as diabetes and arthritis; cayenne improves blood circulation; the bitter, slightly sour flavor of sunflower seeds benefits the spleen and pancreas.*

Place the mesclun greens in the center of a serving plate, top with radish slices, and drizzle on the dressing. Surround the greens with tangerine slices and sprinkle with sunflower seeds.

PURPLE TOP TURNIP (REITICH)
Serves 4

This was my mother's best dish. She learned it from her mother who learned it from her mother back in the old country, Russia. The ratio is about 3 or 4 parts turnip to 1 part onion.

1½ cups purple top turnip

½ cup sweet or Vidalia onion

½ cup finely chopped cilantro or parsley
Sea salt to taste
3 TB olive oil

Use the medium size holes of a 4-sided grater.

Grate the turnip and onion and place in a ceramic or glass bowl.

Mix in the parsley or cilantro and blend in the salt and olive oil.

Let flavors mingle for at least 30 minutes before serving.

Serve as a side dish or a filling for an open-face sandwich.

Dash of Wisdom

Turnip balances blood sugar levels and speeds up metabolism; onion, particularly in its raw form, induces sweating and decreases phlegm of the nose and throat; parsley and cilantro aid in digestion.*

BABY SPINACH AND EDIBLE FLOWERS

Flowers provide not only visual beauty; they are food for the body and soul. Flower essences have the ability to relax our mind and to stimulate and strengthen our immune system.

Nasturtium has a mild peppery taste. Gardenia has a slightly sweet and bitter flavor.

Dash of Wisdom

Nasturtium strengthens the heart; gardenia breaks up toxic accumulation.

3 cups baby spinach leaves
Organic nasturtium and gardenia flowers
1/3 cup tamari roasted pumpkin seeds (pg. 131)

Dressing

3 TB olive oil
2 TB balsamic vinegar
Few pinches sea salt

Gently rinse the spinach and flowers and pat dry.

Place the spinach in a large bowl and blend in the dressing. Add the pumpkin seeds and toss. Transfer to a serving platter and garnish with the flowers.

PRESSED SALAD

Serves 4 or more

1 cup napa (Chinese) cabbage, thinly sliced or grated
½ cup purple onions, thinly sliced
1 cup chopped cilantro or parsley
1 tsp. sea salt, umeboshi plum paste, or ½ cup Umeboshi vinegar

Dash of Wisdom

Fermented foods aid in digestion and help balance the slightly acid forming properties of rice.

Place cabbage, onions and cilantro/parsley in a pickle press or a medium size bowl. Add salt or umeboshi and toss well.

If using a pickle press, screw down the top. If using a bowl, place a plate that fits snuggly on top of the vegetables and add a heavy object on top (such as a rock or a container filled with water). Press the vegetables for at least 30 minutes then drain off the water.

Cooking tip: Vegetables fermented for a longer period become a pickle. Leave them to press for 3 or 4 days, draining off the liquid at least once a day.

SEA VEGETABLES

Sea vegetables provide 80 percent of Earth's oxygen, while they provide us with innumerable healing and beauty benefits. They contain the greatest amount and broadest range of minerals of any life form. They are especially abundant in calcium, iron, and iodine. Hijiki, arame, and wakame, for example, each contain more than ten times the calcium of milk; hijiki contains ten times the amount of iron as meat. All sea vegeta-bles (like all green leafy land vegetables) provide an excellent source of chlorophyll and vitamin D. In general, sea vegetables detoxify the liver, normalize blood sugar levels, lower cholesterol and fat in the blood, aid in weight loss, reduce tumors, alleviate high blood pressure, build bones and teeth, sooth the nerves, and promote glossy hair, a clear complexion, and soft, wrinkle-free skin.*

In current times, more than ever before, sea vegetables should be included in our daily diet. They are our protection against radiation and toxic wastes—they absorb toxins and convert a certain amount to harmless salts.* For this reason, in Japan, seaweed was consumed in great amounts along with miso after the atomic bombings ending World War II and the Chernobyl nuclear meltdown in Russia. Today, this scenario is being repeated again—however, the majority of their seaweed is now being sourced abroad from unpolluted waters.

On many coastlines, we can find an assortment of seaweed washed up on the shore. Take some home, briefly rinse them, then add them to warm bath water, and soak in their powerful life force. You can also cook your harvested seaweed. Rinse off the salt and remove any stones or dirt, and then air-dry.

ARAME—Macro Style

Serves 4

Arame has a mild flavor and is a good choice for people new to sea vegetables. Hijiki can be substituted for arame.

½ oz. arame
Few dashes tamari
Few dashes mirin
Juice of 1 lemon
Roasted sesame seeds (pg. 131)

Rinse the arame and then soak in enough warm water to cover for 10 minutes. Discard soaking water (or feed it to your plants).

Add all ingredients to a sauce pan with enough fresh water to cover by half. Cover and simmer for 10 minutes. Remove and drain.

Either chop arame into bite-size pieces or leave whole.

Place in a large bowl or individual serving bowls and sprinkle roasted sesame seeds on top.

Serve as part of a macrobiotic meal with a grain, beans, dark leafy greens, and a raw salad.

If using hijiki, soak in cold water to cover for 10 minutes. Discard soaking water and prepare same as above.

Cooking tip: Sprinkle cooked arame or hijiki into noodle or grain salads, or toss soaked arame or hijiki into stir-fry dishes.

DULSE AND SPROUT SANDWICH WITH ALMOND ORANGE DRESSING

Dash of Wisdom

During the sprouting process, vitamin and enzyme content increase dramatically, which essentially predigests the nutrients, thereby making it easier to metabolize.

Highest quality breads are chemical-free, no yeast, and made with the fewest organic ingredients. Choose bread made with stone ground flour that is ground from sprouted whole grains. These breads are chewier, tastier, more filling, and will not cause a spike in blood sugar levels.

Alfalfa, in particular, is highly energizing as its root reaches 100 feet into the earth, extracting a wider range of minerals and trace elements than other plants.*

2 slices whole grain bread
Handful alfalfa sprouts
Dulse flakes or roasted whole dulse, crushed

Almond orange dressing

4 oz. soft or silken tofu
1 tsp. light colored miso
Juice of 1 large orange

1 tsp. almond butter or 1 TB almonds finely chopped

Steam tofu for 15 minutes and then drain.

Dilute miso in orange juice.

Purée all ingredients in a blender or blend by hand.

Spread the dressing on the bread, then add the sprouts, and sprinkle with dulse.

ROASTED LAVER AND TOMATO SANDWICH

Roasting imparts a crunchy texture and a fish-like taste.

In a fry pan, briefly roast strips of laver until crispy. Drizzle oil on a slice of whole grain bread, add slices of tomato, and top with crispy laver.

BLANCHED LAVER AND SHOYU

Serves 4

Laver, also called wild Atlantic nori, is the unprocessed form of nori. It has the highest protein content of all seaweed.

Soak laver in enough water to cover until soft. Blanch in its soaking water for around 30 seconds, then immediately drain, and place in a bowl. Sprinkle with shoyu and roasted sesame seeds. Save the cooking water for soup broth or serve as tea.

BROWN RICE NORI ROLL

The Japanese traditionally prepare nori rolls with umeboshi plum or a pickled vegetable when traveling. The salt acts as a preservative and so the food stays fresh for days. Other condiments such as lightly steamed julienne carrots, half-moon cucumber slices, avocado slices, and/or thinly sliced raw scallions add color and texture. Wasabi mustard or yellow mustard contribute a tangy flavor. A bamboo sushi mat makes it easier to roll the nori, but it can also be rolled by hand.

1. Place nori sheet, shiny side down, on the mat. Spread about ½ cup cooled, cooked brown rice evenly across the bottom of the nori leaving a little space uncovered at the bottom.
2. Make a groove in the center of the rice and arrange the fillings inside, and then spread a thin layer of umeboshi paste or mustard across the rice.
3. Using your fingers, wet the top end of the nori with water or shoyu and then begin rolling in a jellyroll fashion.
4. Roll tightly with firm pressure, lapping over moistened end of nori to seal. Firm up the ends of the roll by tapping with your hand while the mat is still wrapped around the sushi.
5. Remove sushi mat and place the roll seam side down until ready to cut.

6. Moisten a sharp, straight-blade knife with water and then slice carefully into a few bite-size equal pieces. Moisten knife repeatedly for smooth cut and finish.
7. Alternatively, place rice in one corner of the nori sheet, add any fillings or condiments you like, and begin rolling, folding the sides in as you go to form a neat little package.

SWEET ADUKI BEAN ASPIC
Serves 6
2 cups cooked aduki beans (pgs. 71–73)
Juice of 1 large lemon
3 drops stevia dark concentrate or 1 TB syrup of choice
1 cup water
3 TB agar flakes, dissolved in 5 TB room temperature water
In a blender, purée the first 4 ingredients until smooth. Combine the mixture and the agar in a pot and simmer until it begins to thicken, stirring continuously. Turn the mixture into a pre-moistened shallow glass or ceramic mold. Set until firm. Refrigerate for faster results. Cut into squares and serve as a side dish or dessert.

CUCUMBER AND WAKAME SALAD
Serves 4
Wakame is a mild, tender sea vegetable that is often added to miso soup. It is sold in both strip form and flakes.
½ cup dry wakame flakes
2 cucumbers
4 scallions
Dressing
Juice of 1 large lemon
2 TB sesame oil
1 tsp. shoyu or tamari
½ tsp. finely grated ginger root
2 drops stevia dark concentrate, or barley malt, or rice syrup to taste
Soak wakame for 10 minutes, then drain. Reserve the soaking water for soup stock (or feed to your plants).
Cut the cucumbers in half, and then slice into thin half moons.
Cut the scallions into thin diagonal slices.
Place wakame in a serving bowl with the cucumbers and scallions and blend in the dressing.

GRAINS AND NOODLES

Refer to pages 67–69 for grain preparation and cooking instructions.

BROWN RICE AND SESAME SALT

Serves 4

2 cups cooked brown rice

1/3 cup sesame salt (pg. 121)

Top each serving with a scant teaspoon of sesame salt; or put the sesame salt in a small bowl and place it in the middle of the table.

Dash of Wisdom

Brown rice is both hypoallergenic and a strengthening food. In Oriental medicine, it is used for the treatment of diabetes.

Serving suggestion: For a balanced and colorful meal, serve with Miso Soup (pg. 84), Cinnamon Scented String Beans (pg. 113), Leafy Greens and Shallots (pg. 88), and Tarty Steamed Beets (pg. 95).

CHESTNUTS AND SWEET BROWN RICE

Serves 6

Chestnuts add a sweet flavor while sweet brown rice contributes a glutinous texture. This combination makes a perfect stuffing for winter squash.

2 cups sweet brown rice

1 cup short or medium grain brown rice

1 cup dried chestnuts

¼ tsp. sea salt

Dash of Wisdom

The chestnut is more like a grain than a nut. It is high in complex carbohydrates and protein, low in fat and calories, and gluten-free. Sweet brown rice is easy to digest.

Soak rice and chestnuts together in two times water to cover overnight. Drain and rinse.

Pressure cooked method: In a large pot, add 4 cups water and all ingredients. Bring to pressure and simmer for around 40 minutes. Turn off the heat and allow the pressure to come down naturally. Uncover and let the steam escape.

Pot method: Add 4½ cups water and all ingredients to the pot, cover, bring to a boil, and simmer for 1 hour.

SIMPLY MILLET

Serves around 4

The ratio is 1 part millet to 3 parts water. Simmer millet with a pinch sea salt for around 35 minutes or until it begins to stick to the bottom of the pot.

Dash of Wisdom

Because of its alkalizing properties, millet is often cooked with little or no salt.*

Serve alone or as a bed for sautéed vegetables, as a stuffing, or add to soups or stews.

Roasted millet: For a fluffier texture, dry roast the millet in the cooking pot on medium to low heat until fragrant, then add the appropriate ratio of boiling water and cook as above.

MILLET, TEFF, YAMS, AND ONIONS

Serves 6

4 ½ cups water
1 cup millet
½ cup teff berries
2 yams
1 onion, diced
¼ tsp. sea salt

Scrub the yams, and then cut into small cubes. In a pot, simmer all ingredients for around 30 minutes or until all water is absorbed, and then gently blend with a rice paddle.

BARLEY SALAD

Serves 6

2 cups cooked whole barley
1 small fennel bulb with fronds; or 1 celery stalk with leaves
1 carrot, diced
1 cup sweet or red onion, diced
1 yellow or red bell pepper, diced
Handful fresh dill, snipped

Dressing

4 TB sesame, olive, argan or sacha inchi oil
Juice of ½ lemon
2 TB brown rice or balsamic vinegar
¼ tsp. cumin powder
3 drops stevia dark concentrate
¼ tsp. sea salt

Dash of Wisdom

Barley strengthens the spleen and pancreas and benefits the gallbladder and nerves; bell peppers improve circulation; and dill calms the mind.*

Place the cooked barley in a large bowl.

Dice the fennel bulb or celery; mince the fronds or leaves.

Simmer carrots until tender in enough water to cover by half, and then drain. (The cooking water makes a nice tea.)

Blend all salad ingredients together then gently blend in the dressing.

Allow flavors to mingle for 30 minutes or longer at room temperature.

Adjust to taste if necessary. It may need more lemon juice or vinegar.

QUINOA TABOULI STUFFED PEPPER

Serves 2 to 4

Roasted quinoa has a nutty taste and a light, crunchy texture.

2 large red bell peppers
¾ cup quinoa, rinsed well through a strainer
1½ cups water

Sea salt

2 cups cilantro or parsley, minced

2 TB whole black peppercorns

Dressing

Juice of 2 large lemons

¼ cup oil of choice

2 or 3 drops stevia dark concentrate

Cut the pepper in half either lengthwise or widthwise. Remove the seeds and the stem area.

Boil the water with a few pinches sea salt.

While the water is boiling, dry roast the quinoa in the cooking pot on medium low heat, shaking frequently until the seeds are dry and fragrant.

Add the boiling water to the roasted quinoa, cover, and simmer for about 15 to 20 minutes, until the water is completely absorbed and the quinoa begins to stick to the bottom of the pot.

Remove the cover and let the steam escape, gently fluff, and then transfer to a large bowl to cool.

Add the cilantro/parsley and peppercorns to the cooled quinoa and blend in the dressing.

Fill each pepper half with the quinoa tabouli.

Cooking tips: Quinoa's protective covering, called saponin, has a bitter flavor and must be rinsed off; quinoa quadruples in size when cooked.

WHEAT BERRY, CRANBERRY, AND SESAME SEED SALAD

Serves 4

Spelt or kamut can be substituted for wheat.

2 cups cooked wheat berries

½ cup unsweetened dry cranberries

Few TB roasted black or tan sesame seeds

½ cup minced cilantro

¼ cup Cinnamon dressing (pg. 96)

Place salad ingredients in a large bowl and blend in the dressing.

Dash of Wisdom

According to Oriental medicine, wheat nurtures the heart-mind; cranberry targets the kidneys.

BUCKWHEAT GROUTS AND PASTA BOWS (KASHA VARNISHKAS)

Serves 4 to 6

This Jewish specialty dish has a warming quality and is therefore appropriate for cold weather.

2 cups cooked whole wheat pasta bows

1 cup roasted buckwheat grouts

2 TB sesame oil

1 onion, diced

Dash of Wisdom

Toasting buckwheat makes it an alkalizing grain.*

Half small head of green or red cabbage
Few pinches sea salt
2 cups boiling water
1 TB tamari
1 cup chopped parsley or cilantro

Cut the cabbage in half; remove the core, and then grate.

In a large fry pan, heat the oil and sauté the onions briefly until translucent. Mix in the cabbage and sea salt and sauté for about 2 minutes, adding enough water to prevent burning.

Blend in the buckwheat grouts. Add the boiling water and tamari, cover, and simmer for 25 to 30 minutes or until all water is absorbed.

Transfer to a large bowl and fold in the pasta bows and parsley/cilantro.

ARMENIAN COUSCOUS AND GARBANZO BEAN SALAD

Serves 4

Whole wheat couscous is made from pre-cooked and coarsely ground whole durum wheat. The refined variety is made from semolina.

1½ cups water
1 cup whole wheat couscous
Few pinches sea salt
Few pinches ground cinnamon
1 cup cooked garbanzo beans (pgs. 71–73)
½ cup minced mint leaves

Dressing

⅓ cup olive oil
⅓ cup lemon juice
3 or 4 drops stevia dark concentrate
Sea salt to taste

Bring water to a boil, stir in the couscous, sea salt, and cinnamon, cover, and simmer for a minute, and then remove from the heat. Wait 15 to 20 minutes until the water is absorbed, then uncover and let the steam escape.

Fluff and transfer to a large bowl to cool. Mix in the beans and mint, and then gently blend in the dressing.

VEGETABLE STIR-FRIED RICE

Serves 4

2 cups cooked brown rice
2 TB sesame oil
1 onion, diced
Minced garlic cloves to taste
2 TB tamari

2 TB mirin
1 celery stalk diced; leaves chopped
1 red or orange bell pepper, diced
¼ cup dulse flakes or roasted dulse, crushed (pg. 121)
Variations: Grated ginger, mushrooms, carrots, broccoli; spices such as cayenne, turmeric, roasted cumin seeds.

Heat sesame oil in a wok. Stir-fry onions and garlic until onions turn translucent. Blend in the tamari and mirin. Add the diced celery and bell pepper and stir-fry for a few minutes.

Mix in the rice and celery leaves, stir to combine, and heat briefly.

Transfer to a bowl and gently blend in the dulse. Serve immediately.

UDON NOODLES WITH GARLIC, BASIL, AND CAPERS
Serves 2
Udon noodles are a Japanese staple made from whole wheat flour.
8 oz. udon noodles (cook according to package instructions)
1 TB light sesame oil
1 TB shoyu
1 TB dark sesame oil
Several garlic cloves, thinly sliced
1 TB sesame oil
⅓ cup fresh basil, chopped
Capers to taste, rinsed well

Place cooked noodles in a large serving bowl. Blend in light sesame oil and shoyu.

Heat dark sesame oil in a skillet; add the garlic and sauté briefly.

Turn off the heat, toss in the cooked noodles, basil, and capers.

Serve immediately.

Cooking tip: Noodles are finished cooking when the center and outside are the same color.

LEGUMES

Beans look like the kidneys and according to both Chinese traditional medicine and the Law of Similarities—beans are the proper food for the kidneys. They are also perfect for diabetics. Because of their high protein content, they help regulate blood sugar while their diuretic and drying properties help balance those who are overweight.

For bean preparation and cooking instructions, refer to pages 69–71. For flavoring with miso, refer to page 49.

SOUPS AND STEWS

For best taste, allow flavors to mingle before serving.

MUNG BEAN SOUP

Serves 4

1 large yam, diced
1 large onion, diced
1 celery stalk with leaves
3–4 cups water
1 cup dry mung beans
3-inch strip kombu, rinsed
¼ tsp. turmeric powder
2 tsp. stevia leaf
2 TB light miso
Fresh lemon juice

Dash of Wisdom

Mung bean belongs to the kidney bean family and is the most alkalizing of all beans: it detoxifies the body; nurtures the gallbladder and liver; and because of its cooling nature, it is used to treat high blood pressure.*

Dice the yams, onions, and celery.

Mince the celery leaves and set aside for garnish. Wash the mung beans; soak the kombu.

In a soup pot or pressure cooker, add the first 8 ingredients. Cook the mung beans until they become creamy.

Add diluted miso and simmer a few minutes.

Add a splash of lemon juice to individual servings and garnish with minced celery leaves.

Cooking tip: Mung beans do not need pre-soaking; however, to speed up the cooking time, soak in boiling hot water to generously cover for 1 hour, and then drain and rinse.

SPLIT PEA AND BARLEY STEW

Serves 5

½ cup whole barley
1 cup split peas
3-inch strip kombu, soaked
2 TB stevia leaf
2 TB grated ginger root
½ tsp. turmeric
Pinch cayenne pepper
2 TB tamari
2 large lemons
Handful cilantro or parsley, minced

Dash of Wisdom

Split pea is healing to the liver, spleen, and pancreas; turmeric protects the liver from toxins, lowers cholesterol, dissolves gallstones and aids in the digestion of protein.

For sauté

1 TB dark sesame oil

3–6 garlic cloves, chopped

2 onions, diced

2 carrots, diced

Soak barley and peas separately overnight, then drain and rinse. In a soup pot or pressure cooker, add kombu and its soaking water, then the barley and peas and enough water to cover by 1 inch.

Bring to a boil, stir in the stevia, ginger, turmeric, and cayenne. Cover and simmer.

Heat the oil and sauté the garlic, onions, and carrots. Add just enough water if necessary to prevent burning. Add to the pot, stir and continue simmering until peas are 80 percent cooked.

Stir in the tamari and cook until beans are soft.

Add a splash of lemon juice in each serving bowl and garnish with cilantro or parsley.

ADUKI BEAN AND SQUASH SOUP

Serves 4 to 6

1 cup aduki beans

1 butternut squash

3-inch strip kombu, soaked

2-inch piece ginger root

4 cups water

1 TB coriander seeds

1 TB stevia leaves

½ tsp. cumin powder

2 TB chickpea miso

Dash of Wisdom

Aduki bean is healing to the kidney, heart, and small intestines; the combination of ginger, coriander, and cumin help diminish flatulence.*

Soak aduki beans overnight. Rinse and drain. Clean and cut squash into cubes.

Peel and finely grate the ginger root.

In a soup pot, add water and all ingredients except the miso, and simmer until the beans are soft. Remove the kombu and cut into small squares, and then return to the pot. Dilute the miso, add back to the pot, and gently simmer for a few minutes.

LENTIL, YAM, AND KALE SOUP

Serves 4 to 6

4 cups water

1 cup brown or green lentils

3-inch strip kombu, soaked

1 large yam, diced

1 large onion, diced

2 TB stevia leaves

Dash of Wisdom

Lentil promotes circulation, which benefits the heart*; the yam, which looks like the pancreas, also strengthens the pancreas; bay leaf aids in digestion.

1 or 2 bay leaves
2 pinches ground nutmeg
Several kale leaves, chopped
2 TB chickpea or brown rice miso
Several garlic cloves, minced

Simmer first 8 ingredients until lentils are soft.

Remove bay leaves, add the kale, and simmer for 5 minutes.

Dilute the miso, stir back into the pot, and simmer a few minutes more.

Sprinkle minced garlic on top of each serving bowl.

SAVORY DISHES

CINNAMON SCENTED STRING BEANS
Serves 4

1 lb. string beans
Sea salt
1–2 TB cinnamon
2 tsp. olive oil
Several garlic cloves, thinly sliced

Dash of Wisdom

The string bean strengthens the pancreas and kidneys*; a half teaspoon of cinnamon daily is reputed to lower both blood sugar and cholesterol levels.

Clean and trim beans.

Steam until tender/crunchy then remove immediately to a bowl.

Blend in a few pinches sea salt and cinnamon.

Stir-fry garlic in oil for a couple of minutes, and then blend with the beans.

BLACK BEAN AND FENNEL SALAD
Serves 4 to 6

Dash of Wisdom

Fennel helps expel gas.

Salad ingredients

2 cups cooked black beans
1 carrot diced and blanched
1 fennel bulb diced; fronds minced
1 purple onion, diced
Several red radishes, thinly sliced
2 TB roasted fennel seeds (pg. 131)
¼ tsp. sea salt

Dressing

⅓ cup sesame or olive oil
3 TB brown rice vinegar
Juice of 1 lemon
3 or 4 drops stevia dark concentrate

Combine all salad ingredients and blend in the dressing.

Allow flavors to marinate for at least 30 minutes before serving.
If necessary, add more lemon juice.

PINTO BEANS AND AMARANTH
Serves 4 to 6
2 cups cooked pinto beans
3 cups water
1 cup amaranth, rinsed
1 ½ cups corn kernels
¼ tsp. sea salt
Several scallions, thinly sliced on the diagonal
Simmer amaranth, corn, and sea salt for 15 minutes.
Add scallions and continue cooking for a few minutes more.
Blend together with the pinto beans.

LENTIL CROQUETTES WITH MUSTARD DRESSING
Yields around 8
2 cups cooked brown lentils
4 TB whole wheat or buckwheat flour
1 tsp. light sesame oil for sautéing
1 onion, diced
1 carrot, diced
Handful parsley or cilantro, finely chopped

Dash of Wisdom

Mustard has a stimulating effect on the lungs, which in turn, helps discharge phlegm.*

Liquid ingredients
Juice of 1 large lemon
3 drops stevia dark concentrate
1 tsp. tamari
Preheat oven to 350°F.
In a large bowl, mash the lentils and blend in the flour.
Sauté the onions and carrots for a minute, then add the parsley/cilantro.
Add the liquid ingredients and continue sautéing until liquid is absorbed, then blend with the lentils and flour.
Form into patties and bake until browned, around 30 minutes.
Serve with Mustard Dressing.
Mustard dressing
Blend together:
¼ cup vinegar plus 1 TB water
2–4 drops stevia dark concentrate
1 tsp. mustard powder

MINTY CHICKPEA SALAD WITH PUMPKIN OIL DRESSING

Serves 4

During one of my cooking classes, one gentleman exclaimed, "This is the best thing I've eaten since I left home!" It was the pumpkin oil. It is the gourmet touch not only in salad dressings, but also drizzled on pasta, vegetables, and bread.

Salad ingredients

2 cups cooked chickpeas

1 cup diced carrots

1 cup diced sweet or red onion

1 large celery stalk, diced and the leaves minced

½ cup minced mint leaves

Dressing

3 TB pumpkin oil

2 TB vinegar

2–4 drops stevia dark concentrate

Juice of 1 lemon

Sea salt to taste

In a small saucepan, blanch carrots in half cup water for 2 minutes, then drain. Combine salad ingredients in a large serving bowl and gently fold in the dressing.

Adjust seasonings to taste. Allow flavors to blend for 30 minutes before serving.

PAN FRIED TOFU WITH CHINESE GINGER SAUCE

Serves 2 to 4

Serve as a main course accompanied with a grain and a leafy green vegetable.

½ lb. extra firm tofu

2 TB sesame oil

Tamari

Slice tofu in half depth-wise, and then slice both sections in half.

In a large fry pan, heat the oil and then add the tofu slices.

Spoon a splash of tamari on top of each slice and sear until

the tofu begins to brown, adding just enough water to prevent burning.

Repeat with the other side, and then transfer to a serving plate.

Ginger sauce

2 TB kuzu or arrowroot

¾ cup water

1 TB umeboshi paste

Couple splashes tamari

2 TB mirin

2 TB finely grated ginger root

In a small bowl, dilute kuzu or arrowroot in 6 TB water, then blend in the rest of the ingredients.

Simmer in a sauce pan for a few minutes, stirring continuously until the sauce thickens.

Pour over the tofu triangles and serve immediately.

Cooking tip: Use the ginger sauce to enliven steamed or sautéed vegetables.

SWEET AND SPICY TOFU TRIANGLES

Serves 2 to 4

Serve as a main course or sandwich filling, or slice into smaller triangles and add to stir-fries or a leaf lettuce salad.

½ lb. extra firm tofu

2 TB red palm, coconut, or sesame oil

Dressing

3 TB shoyu or tamari plus 1 tsp. water to dilute

3 drops stevia dark concentrate

Cayenne pepper to taste

Dash of Wisdom

Tofu's cooling properties helps lower high blood pressure, but only in moderate amounts—when consumed regularly it weakens the kidneys.*

Slice tofu in half depth-wise, and then slice both sections in half.

In a large heavy skillet, heat oil to hot. Add the tofu and sear for 1 minute. If necessary, work in batches so that each slice fits comfortably in the skillet to ensure even cooking.

Reduce heat and add about a teaspoon of dressing on top using the back side of the spoon to coat evenly.

Fry until crispy, then repeat with the other side.

Remove to a cutting board and slice each of the 4 sections on the diagonal to form 8 triangles.

SCRAMBLED TOFU, MUSHROOMS, AND ONIONS

Serves 4

Serve for breakfast with whole grain toast or for lunch or dinner with a soup and a grain.

10 oz. soft tofu

2 TB light sesame oil

½ cup diced onions

sea salt

½ cup sliced button mushrooms

Tamari

Few pinches cumin powder

2–3 drops stevia dark concentrate added to ¼ cup water

½ cup minced parsley

Freshly ground peppercorns

Crumble tofu in a bowl.

Sauté the onions with a couple pinches of sea salt for 1 minute. Add the mushrooms, a splash of tamari, and cumin and continue sautéing for a couple of minutes.

Blend in the tofu and stevia water, cover, and simmer for around 5 minutes. Remove the cover and boil off any remaining liquid.

Stir in the parsley and pepper.

TEMPEH WITH TANGY ORANGE SAUCE

Serves 4

Serve as a main course; as a sandwich filling with leaf lettuce; or cut into quarters and add to vegetables, pasta or grain dishes.

1 package tempeh

Dulse flakes or roasted and crushed whole dulse (pg. 121)

Tangy Orange Sauce

⅓ cup orange juice

4 TB mirin

1 TB light miso or 1 TB shoyu

2 TB finely grated ginger root

Dash of Wisdom

Tempeh that is produced in its countries of origin, Thailand and Indonesia, still retains its vitamin B12. However, in the U.S.A., tempeh is manufactured in modern sterile conditions (government required regulations), which destroys its vitamin B12.

Cut tempeh into 4 equal sections, then marinate in sauce for 30 minutes or more.

In a large skillet, add tempeh and marinade, cover, and simmer 5 to 7 minutes or until brown, then repeat with the other side.

Add small amounts of orange juice whenever necessary to prevent burning. Remove to a serving plate and top with dulse or laver.

BOSTON BAKED BEANS

Serves around 4

For a well-balanced meal, serve with brown rice sprinkled with sesame salt (pg. 121); a green leafy vegetable; and pickled or fermented vegetables (pg. 98) to aid in digestion.

1 cup dried kidney beans, soaked overnight

3 cups water

3 inch strip kombu, soaked

1 large onion, quartered

Dash of Wisdom

Fresh ginger helps break down high protein foods.

Chunk of ginger root
½ tsp. cinnamon
¼ tsp. ground cloves or nutmeg
2 scant TB chickpea miso

Dressing

1 sweet onion, diced
¼ cup apple cider or brown rice vinegar
2 garlic cloves, finely chopped
1 TB dry mustard
1 TB yacon syrup or few drops stevia dark concentrate
1 tsp. ground black peppercorns

Simmer the first five ingredients until beans are 80 percent cooked.

Add the remaining ingredients, except the miso, and simmer until the beans are soft.

Remove the ginger, kombu, and onion and discard.

Drain the beans, but reserve a little broth to dilute the miso.

Dilute the miso and blend with the dressing ingredients, and then gently fold the mixture in with the beans.

MUNG BEAN NOODLES AND SCALLIONS WITH SESAME CITRUS SAUCE

Serves 4 or more

Mung bean noodles (also called cellophane or transparent noodles) are made from mung bean flour and sold in bundled or strand form. Because they have virtually no flavor on their own, they absorb other flavors. The noodles will keep indefinitely in a tightly covered container stored in a cool dry place.

Dash of Wisdom

Mung bean noodles are an easily digestible and cooling food, and like the mung bean, the noodles are used to treat high blood pressure, anxiety, and to reduce toxicity; oranges are beneficial for diabetes and other highly acidic conditions such as arthritis.*

Half package noodles
Pot of boiled water
1 TB sesame oil
1 cup scallions sliced diagonally
1 red bell pepper, thinly sliced

Sesame citrus sauce

½ cup fresh orange or tangerine juice
1 TB brown sesame paste
1 tsp. light colored syrup
Whole peppercorns to taste

Tie one end of the noodles with a string and soak in enough boiled water to cover for 15 minutes, or until soft.

Rinse under cold water and drain. As they soften, they absorb a large quantity of liquid and become transparent.

With a scissors, cut bean strands into thirds.

Heat oil in a wok, then add the scallions and red peppers.

Stir-fry briefly until soft. Reduce heat, add the noodles, stir to combine, and then blend in the sauce.

Continue cooking until the noodles have absorbed the sauce.

Add more orange juice if necessary.

Transfer to a serving bowl and blend in the peppercorns.

WHITE BEAN PÂTÉ

Yields: 1½ cups

Serve as a side dish, or with crudités, or as an open-face sandwich filling.

1 cup cooked navy, lima, or northern beans

Sauce

2 TB lemon juice

1 TB balsamic or brown rice vinegar

1 TB sweet white or chickpea miso

3–5 garlic cloves, chopped

3 TB chopped fresh basil

1 TB olive, sacha inchi, or argan oil

Freshly ground black peppercorns

Dash of Wisdom

White beans are beneficial for the lungs and large intestine; basil soothes the nerves, treats insomnia, and helps center the mind.*

Place the beans in a large bowl.

Blend miso with lemon juice and vinegar, and then combine with the other sauce ingredients.

Blend the sauce with the beans, then purée mixture in batches in a food processor fitted with an 'S' blade, and pulse until smooth. Add water to blend if necessary.

Adjust to taste—it may require more lemon juice.

Cover and store in the refrigerator for up to 3 days.

CONDIMENTS

STEVIA

Flavor is in the details.

ROASTED WHOLE DULSE

Roasting dulse imparts a smoky flavor, which is similar to bacon, and has virtually no calories.

Roast whole dulse in a skillet over medium heat until crispy.

Crush and sprinkle over salads or any cooked dishes, or on popcorn.

CHIA SPICE

3 TB chia seeds
½ tsp. dulse flakes
2 tsp. cumin powder
Pinch sea salt

Dash of Wisdom

This combination not only provides a wealth of minerals for your body; it is power food for your brain.

In a fry pan, roast chia seeds on low heat until crispy. Remove to a bowl. Roast the dulse flakes until crispy and add to the chia seeds.

Roast the cumin powder and combine with the chia seeds and dulse and then blend in the sea salt.

Cooking tip: Try also chia seeds with cayenne pepper, roasted curry powder, cinnamon, or your favorite spices.

SESAME SALT (GOMASIO)

This tasty Japanese condiment is traditionally served over rice. The surabachi and surikogi, which are similar to a mortar and pestle, can be purchased online. (See Resources chapter for prepared gomasio.) The two varieties of sesame seeds are tan and black. Black seeds have a slightly stronger flavor and are

Dash of Wisdom

Both black and tan seeds strengthen the liver and kidneys. Although tan seeds have the same properties as black seeds, they are milder-acting.

sold only in the unhulled form. Tan seeds are sold both hulled and unhulled. The unhulled forms are rich in calcium (90 mg. per tablespoon vs. 10 mg. for hulled), iron, and phosphorus.

The ratio is 75 percent sesame seeds to 25 percent sea salt. For best results, use sea salt crystals. Roast the seeds and sea salt separately, then combine both in a surabachi and grind in a continuous clockwise, spiral direction until the seeds are about 80 percent ground.

Store in a glass jar in the refrigerator.

Cooking tip: The nutrients of sesame seeds are better absorbed if they are roasted, ground, or pulverized before consumption.

MISO MUSTARD

2 tsp. light miso
¼ cup brown mustard

Blend miso and mustard until smooth. Use as a spreading for sandwiches or for brown rice nori rolls, as a dip for raw vegetables, or to enliven steamed vegetables.

(*Compliments from the website of Eden Foods.*)

GRATED DAIKON RADISH

Serve as an accompaniment to beans or fish.
Finely grate one daikon radish.

For single servings, place 1 tablespoon on the serving plate and add a splash of shoyu or tamari on top. For family style, place in a small bowl in the center of the table and add a splash of tamari on top.

Dash of Wisdom
Daikon helps the body discharge old animal protein and fats; helps digest beans; and diminishes appetite.

DESSERTS

These desserts are so nutritious, you can eat dessert first!

BLUEBERRY COUSCOUS CAKE AND BLUEBERRY MOUSSE

Serves 4

Substitute any fruit of the season.

The cake

2 cups water

2 cups whole wheat couscous

Juice of 1 lemon

1 TB syrup of choice

Pinch sea salt

Dash of Wisdom

The color blue has antioxidant protection particularly beneficial to the brain. Raw blueberries have the highest amount—nearly 60 times the recommended daily levels. So do not overindulge.

Bring water to a boil in a saucepan.

Add the couscous, cover, and simmer for 5 minutes. Turn off the heat, wait 15 minutes, then gently fluff.

Blend in the lemon juice and sweetener.

Rinse a 9-inch glass or ceramic baking dish. Evenly distribute the couscous, then press down firmly.

Allow around 1 hour for the cake to firm, and then spread the mousse evenly over the top.

The mousse

½ cup fresh blueberries

8 oz. soft or silken tofu

1 TB sesame paste

2 TB lemon or lime juice

Syrup of choice to taste

Vegan milk of choice (unsweetened)

Purée all ingredients together adding just enough vegan milk to blend.

CHESTNUT CREAM PIE

Serves 6

2 cups dried chestnuts or 1 lb. fresh chestnuts

Sea salt

Handful roasted almonds or hazelnuts, chopped

Oat Flake Pie Crust (pg. 125)

Dried chestnut procedure

Soak overnight in 2 times water to cover. Drain and discard water.

Cook in 2 times water to cover with a few pinches sea salt until soft.

Remove chestnuts to a chopping board and roughly chop.

Purée with just enough cooking water to achieve a smooth consistency.

Pour filling into Oat Flake Pie Crust and sprinkle nuts on top.

Fresh chestnut procedure

Remove the shells and cook in boiling salted water for ten minutes, and then skim off the skin. Return to a boil, add the spices, and cook until tender when pierced with a fork, then continue as above.

OAT FLAKE PIE CRUST

½ cup oat flakes
2 TB syrup of choice
Dash sea salt
Cinnamon to taste

In a skillet, combine oat flakes, sea salt, and cinnamon. Roast over medium-low heat, shaking frequently to prevent burning.

When oats are beginning to brown and become crisp, blend in the syrup. Gently press the mixture into a 9-inch pie plate.

PUMPKIN PIE

Serves 6

The success of this pie depends on the sweetness of the pumpkin or squash. Choose a pumpkin with raised nodules on the skin, which indicates sweetness and thus a bright orange pulp.

Dash of Wisdom

Pumpkin helps regulate blood sugar levels and benefits the pancreas.*

1 Hokkaido pumpkin or butternut squash
3 oz. soft tofu
1 TB sesame paste
Pinch sea salt
Pinch each: nutmeg, cloves, cinnamon
Sweetener: 2 TB any syrup diluted in 1 cup water or 1 cup stevia marinade (pg. 135)
Oat Flake Pie Crust (see above)

Preheat oven to 350°F.

Remove the seeds and stringy fibers from the pumpkin or squash, and cut into slices.

Steam until soft. Let cool.

Purée all ingredients until smooth.

Taste for sweetness and adjust if necessary.

Pour filling into Oat Flake Pie Crust.

BAKED APPLE

Preheat oven to 350°F.

Choose the smallest, reddest apple.

Remove the core from the top taking care not to pierce the bottom, and then remove the seeds.

Fill the apple with a mixture of grated orange rind, cinnamon, and a pinch of sea salt.

Bake for 30 or 40 minutes.

Dash of Wisdom

Apple contains pectin, which removes cholesterol, toxic metals such as lead and mercury, and residues of radiation; apples are also cleansing and beneficial for the liver and gallbladder, actually softening gallstones.*

APPLE CRISP

Serves 6

6 apples, sliced in half moons
2 TB syrup of choice diluted in half cup water
Pinch sea salt
2 pinches/each cinnamon and nutmeg

The crisp

2 cups rolled oats
½ cup kamut, spelt, or oat flour
¼ cup olive or coconut oil

Preheat oven to 350°F.

Blend together the apples, sweetener, sea salt, and spices and place in a shallow baking dish.

Combine the crisp ingredients in a large bowl and blend. Then spread evenly over the apple mixture.

Bake 30 to 40 minutes or until the crust is golden brown and the apples are juicy.

Cooking tip: 1 medium apple = 1 cup chopped apple
1 lb. apples = 3 cups sliced apples

CINNAMON COOKIES

Yields 15 cookies

Flax seeds are a substitute for egg.

Dry ingredients

1 cup stone ground, whole wheat flour
1 cup oat flour
½ cup ground golden flax seeds
½ tsp. cinnamon

Wet ingredients

½ cup coconut water or unsweetened vegan milk
2 TB sesame paste
⅓ cup soft or silken tofu
⅓ cup syrup of choice
1 tsp. pure vanilla extract

Preheat oven to 350°F.

Mix dry ingredients together in a large bowl.

Mix wet ingredients together in a separate bowl.

Fold wet ingredients into dry ingredients and gently blend.

Lightly oil 2 cookie sheets. Use about 2 TB batter for each cookie. Moisten your hands with water and form into balls and then gently flatten.

Bake for 20 to 30 minutes, until the tops have slightly browned. Remove to a platter and cool.

STEWED FRUIT AND SACHA INCHI SEEDS

Use any combination of seasonal fruits such as mango and papaya or a variety of berries.

1 apple cored and sliced
1 pear cored and sliced
Pinch sea salt
2 pinches each cinnamon and cloves
Garnish: roasted sacha inchi seeds

Dash of Wisdom

Fruit digests better with the addition of the spices; sacha inchi seed is high in protein with a near 1:1 ratio of omega-3 and -6 EFAs, which is crucial in the transport and breakdown of cholesterol.

Simmer fruit, spices, and sea salt in a few tablespoons of water. As the fruits cook, they release their water. Simmer until soft, adding a little more water if necessary to prevent burning. Top each serving with a sprinkle of sacha inchi seeds.

FRUIT KANTEN

Kanten is the Japanese name for agar seaweed. Prepared in this way, it is a healthy substitute for jello gelatin (an animal by-product).

2 cups any seasonal fruit or combination
3 TB agar flakes
3 cups unprocessed apple juice
2 pinches each: nutmeg and cinnamon

Dash of Wisdom

Agar is calorie-free and healing to the liver, heart, and lungs.*

Finely chop the fruit.
Combine all ingredients in a saucepan and bring to a near boil, stirring frequently. Reduce heat and simmer until agar flakes have dissolved, about 10 minutes.
Rinse a glass or ceramic mold and add the kanten. Set until gelled. Refrigerate for faster results. Cut into squares and serve.

PURPLE RICE COCONUT PUDDING

Serves 4

Purple rice (or black rice) originates from Asia. It has a slightly sweet taste and glutinous texture.

1 cup purple rice
3 cups coconut water
2 ripe bananas, sliced
Few pinches sea salt
Unsweetened coconut flakes
Cinnamon

Dash of Wisdom

Black rice nourishes the kidney; banana detoxifies the body; and, in China, because of its high potassium content, it is used to reduce high blood pressure.*

Bring first 4 ingredients to a boil. Lower heat and simmer for about 40 to 50 minutes, until liquid is absorbed.
Garnish each bowl with coconut flakes and cinnamon. Serve warm or cool.

Cooking tip: Because coconut water, bananas, and purple rice are naturally sweet, additional sweetener is not necessary.

CREAMY PEACH-LIME COBBLER

Serves 6

2½ TB arrowroot or kuzu
4 peaches, sliced
1 cup unsweetened coconut milk
Juice of 1 lime and few gratings of zest
Syrup of choice to taste, or few drops stevia dark concentrate
Pinch sea salt
Pinch ground cloves
Oat Flake Pie Crust (pg. 125)

Dash of Wisdom

Because of its cooling nature, the peach is effective in relieving high blood pressure.*

Thoroughly dissolve arrowroot/kuzu in half cup room temperature water. In a saucepan, combine the rest of the ingredients and bring to a slow boil. Lower heat and simmer until peaches are soft.

Stir the arrowroot/ kuzu again, add to the pot, and bring back to a slow boil. Reduce heat and simmer for a few minutes, stirring continuously until the sauce thickens.

When cooled, pour into Oat Flake Pie Crust.

PUDDING WITH PEAR GINGER SAUCE

Serves 4 to 6

Puddings can be prepared with either freshly made or leftover grain.

Dash of Wisdom

In the Orient, the pear is used for diabetics because of its slightly sour flavor.

2 cups cooked grain
½ to 1 cup unsweetened vegan milk
1 TB sesame paste (optional)

Purée all ingredients until smooth and place in single serving bowls.

Pear ginger sauce

¼ cup lemon juice or water
2 or 3 ripe pears, cored and sliced
Pinch sea salt
2 TB finely grated ginger root
1–2 TB syrup of choice, or a 3–5 drops of stevia concentrate
1 TB sesame paste (optional)

In a saucepan, add all ingredients and simmer until soft.

Purée mixture in a blender. If necessary, adding just enough water to blend. Spread evenly over the pudding.

BAKED PLANTAIN

Serves 6

2 large, ripe plantains

Preheat oven to 350°F.

Wash and dry the plantains in their skin. Trim off both ends and make a slit lengthwise.

Place them on a baking sheet and bake for approximately 45 minutes (turning over halfway through the baking), until the plantain flesh is tender.

Slice each plantain into thirds and serve in the skin.

Dash of Wisdom

Researchers in India have shown that psyllium husk, which is the outer layer of the plantain seed, can significantly reduce cholesterol when administered to patients with type 2 diabetes.

TEFFIOCA CHOCOLATE PUDDING

Serves 4

Teff grains cook to a gelatin type consistency in about 20 minutes.

2 ½ cups coconut water or unsweetened vegan milk

½ cup teff (cooks at a 4:1 ratio with liquid)

3 tsp. cacao powder

Syrup of choice to taste

Cinnamon

In a saucepan, bring 2 cups of the liquid ingredient and teff to a boil. Lower the heat and add the remaining ingredients. Cover and simmer until the liquid is absorbed, stirring occasionally.

Let mixture cool to room temperature.

Purée until smooth with enough remaining liquid to attain the consistency you prefer.

Garnish each bowl generously with cinnamon.

SNACKS

NUTS AND SEEDS

Nuts and seeds are the essence of the plant for they contain all nutrients in a concentrated form; they are high in both protein and fatty acids and are typically the highest source of vitamin E.* Eat sparingly, one-by-one. Roasting and/or soaking overnight will reduce the effects of rancidity while it also cuts down on the oiliness, making them more digestible.

Dash of Wisdom

Hulled and shelled seeds and nuts become rancid almost immediately; rancidity affects the liver and gallbladder and irritates the stomach and intestines.*

Roasting procedure—Add just enough nuts or seeds to fit comfortably in a skillet. Roast over low to medium-low heat, shaking often to prevent burning. When they are fragrant and crisp, they are done. Remove immediately to a bowl.

Cooking tip: Moisten your index finger, gather some seeds on it, and taste for doneness—they should be crisp.

TAMARI ROASTED PUMPKIN SEEDS

Roast seeds until they begin to pop. Then add a few splashes of shoyu or tamari, coat evenly with a wooden spoon, and continue roasting briefly until dry. Enjoy alone or sprinkle on salads, grains, or vegetable dishes or as a garnish for puréed soups.

Dash of Wisdom

Pumpkin seeds benefit the colon, pancreas and spleen.* Recommended specifically for impotency and swollen prostate with signs of urination problems.*

SPICY SUNFLOWER AND CUMIN SEEDS

Roast sunflower seeds and cumin seeds separately.

Place in a bowl, lightly sprinkle with ground cayenne pepper, and blend well.

Dash of Wisdom

Cayenne pepper is used as prevention against strokes, to disperse stagnant blood (blood clotting), and is one of the highest botanical sources of vitamin C.*

ROASTED POMEGRANATE SEEDS

A small bowlful of roasted pomegranate seeds makes an unusual and delectable snack or dessert.

Remove the seeds from the pomegranate, then rinse and dry.

Roast in a skillet on low heat until fragrant.

Dash of Wisdom

Pomegranate seeds aid in digestion.

Cooking tip: Serve alone, or combine with yacon dried slices or other dried fruit, and any variety of roasted seeds or nuts.

CRUDITÉS WITH DIP

Cut up fresh vegetables such as bell peppers, celery, cucumbers, Jerusalem artichoke, jicama, turnip, carrot, rutabaga, and daikon radish. Serve with Tofu Dill Sour Cream (pg. 87) or White Bean Pâté (pg. 119).

CHIA CHIPS

The seeds can be sprinkled directly on foods or ground in a pepper mill or coffee grinder.

4 TB chia seeds
1 cup water
1 TB curry powder
¼ tsp. sea salt

Dash of Wisdom

Chia's gel or mucilage acts as a nonirritating, natural laxative.

Combine chia seeds and water in a bowl and wait 15 minutes or more until the seeds blossom and turn gelatinous.
Blend with the curry powder.
Cover a cookie sheet with parchment paper to prevent burning or brush with oil, and then spread a thin layer of the chia mixture.
Dehydrate at 130°F overnight in the oven or use a traditional dehydrator.

TRAIL MIX

Yields ⅓ cup
Combine equal parts: roasted whole cacao beans or cacao nibs, roasted almonds, and dried goji berries.
Cacao (*theobromine cacao*) is the fruit of the cacao tree that grows in tropical climates where it is usually shaded by coffee bushes. The seeds of the fruit, called cacao beans, are the source of chocolate and all cocoa products. Its taste is somewhat bitter, like bitter chocolate. Roasted cacao beans are slightly sweet and crunchy; raw beans are somewhat more bitter and not as crunchy. (Highest quality cacao beans are reputed to be from Bocas del Toro, Panama.)
Cacao beans are high in minerals and antioxidants. Unlike chocolate, cacao is not addictive and therefore safely satisfies a chocolate craving. (As a cautionary note, the theobromine in the cacao bean has a caffeine effect, and thus acts as a stimulant.)
Almond is the only nut to alkalize the blood, while all others acidify.* The goji berry, also known as Chinese wolfberry, tastes somewhat like raisins. In China, it is used in small amounts to treat diabetes, high blood pressure, poor eyesight, vertigo, and sexual inadequacies. In the West, it is known to be high in antioxidants (and is usually eaten by the handful!).

NORI WITH TERIYAKI SPREAD

Wave nori sheets over a flame until crispy. Cut into squares and lightly brush Teriyaki Spread on top.

Teriyaki spread

1 TB syrup of choice
2 TB shoyu
1 TB brown rice vinegar
1 tsp. finely grated ginger root

Combine all ingredients in a small saucepan and simmer several minutes. As the liquid is reduced, the taste becomes more concentrated. Remove ginger slices and discard.

YACON DRIED SLICES

Similar to dried mango slices, this ready-made snack satisfies a sweet craving while it also lowers blood sugar levels.

ELIXIRS

e.lix.ir/I'liksər/ Noun: A magical or medicinal potion

STEVIA GINGER LEMONADE

This sweet and tangy elixir is calorie-free and curbs the appetite. It is especially beneficial after a meal to aid in digestion.

Stevia options:

3 or 4 stevia teabags

3 tablespoons dried leaf

2 tablespoons dried leaf powder

Dash of Wisdom

Lemon, also lime, lowers blood sugar levels and breaks down fat, which in effect, cleanses the liver; ginger cleanses the blood thereby improving circulation, which includes a bloated feeling.*

To a pot, add a half gallon of water and one of the stevia options above.

If using the dried leaves or powder, either place in a small muslin tea bag or add directly to the pot.

Heat water to near-boiling. (Boiling destroys the plant's fragile enzymes along with its medicinal qualities. It also produces a bitter taste.)

Cool to room temperature, then remove the teabags or strain if using the leaves or powder.

Add a half cup lemon juice and one tablespoon ginger juice. If it is too sweet, add more lemon juice and/or water. Serve chilled or warm.

Ginger juice preparation

A ginger grater is the perfect tool for making ginger juice.

Otherwise, use a garlic press or a fine-size grater. Select a firm ginger root. Grate the ginger, then gather the gratings in your fist and squeeze out the juice. Discard the pulp.

Stevia marinade

To eight ounces of water, add about eight drops stevia dark concentrate, two or more tablespoons lemon juice, and one scant teaspoon ginger juice (optional).

Sparkling ginger lemonade

Use effervescent spring water and prepare as above.

ENZYME-RICH GREEN DRINK

Enzymes are substances that make life possible. They rejuvenate and detoxify the liver and purify the blood. This elixir will keep you youthful, energized, and happy.

DASH OF WISDOM

Micro algae are a highly concentrated source of protein. This special form of protein especially benefits diabetics and others who have eaten too many animal products and refined foods.*

Fresh juice made from acid and subacid fruits lower blood sugar levels. Use carrots or beets instead of fruit to sweeten vegetable juice.

Drink immediately as nutrients begin to degrade twenty minutes after juicing.

Blend together:

Fresh greens: watercress; handful of parsley or cilantro

Couple stalks of celery or a small fennel bulb
One cucumber
One large carrot or beet
Micro-algae: half teaspoon spirulina powder or wild blue-green powder
Peeled fresh ginger root (optional)

HEMP SEED MILK

Hemp seed provides a balanced source of the omega-3 and -6 essential fatty acids. A balanced combination enables you to manage stress better while it also helps reduce hunger. Soak two full tablespoons hulled hemp seeds in sixteen ounces of water for twenty minutes at room temperature. Pulse in a blender and refrigerate.

YACON LEAF TEA

The most powerful medicinal properties of the yacon plant are concentrated in its leaves. Simply by sipping the tea, you lower your blood sugar levels.

Brew one teaspoon yacon tea leaves in one and a half cups near-boiling water. Steep for several minutes. If you like, sweeten with either yacon syrup or stevia teabags. Serve warm or cool.

FENUGREEK SEED TEA

This tea will help balance your blood sugar and cholesterol levels.

Soak one teaspoon of seeds and one licorice root in eight ounces of water overnight. The following morning, remove the licorice root. Drink the water and chew the seeds well.

NOPAL CACTUS TEA

will lower your blood sugar and cholesterol levels.

Bring one and a half cups of water to a boil, add the cactus, cover, and simmer for fifteen minutes. Then drink the water.

HIBISCUS FLOWER TEA

will benefit your kidneys and bladder.

Several hibiscus flowers
8 oz. water
1 slice fresh ginger root
2 whole cloves
1 cinnamon stick

Wash the flowers, and then make an incision around the tough base of the flower (calyx) to free and remove it with the seed capsule attached. In a pot, combine the flowers and the calyx in eight ounces of water and bring to a near-boil.

Remove from the heat and add one slice of fresh ginger, two whole cloves and a cinnamon stick.

Cover the pot and let it steep for fifteen minutes, then drain off the liquid. Serve hot or cold or use the liquid to make a kanten fruit dessert (pg. 127).

ROSEMARY TEA

promotes heightened awareness, which naturally relieves depression.

2 teaspoons dried rosemary or fresh flower tops

1 licorice root

1 cup water

Steep rosemary and licorice root in freshly boiled water for twenty minutes. Drink in small portions throughout the day.

COCONUT WATER

from a freshly picked, young coconut will cleanse your kidneys.

CORN SILK TEA

is traditionally used to treat diabetes and high blood pressure and to improve the function of the kidney and gallbladder.

Remove the corn silk from one ear of corn and simmer in two cups water for several minutes and then strain.

MINT TEA

after a meal will aid in your digestion.

Brew mint leaves alone or with stevia ginger lemonade (pg. 135).

LICORICE TEA

is known as the Elixir of Life. Since earliest recorded history, licorice has been valued as an aphrodisiac and a beautifying agent, and for its ability to promote vitality and longevity.

Add one half to one teaspoon licorice root powder to one cup boiling water; or brew any flower tea with a stick of licorice. Take before meals.

CHLORELLA

is among the most ancient life forms on the earth. This single-celled fresh water algae is virtually unchanged in over two billion years of existence. Thus it harbors the spark that characterized the original creative energy of the planet. When you feel energized, you can overcome stress and mental irritation. Chlorella also contains more chlorophyll than any other food, and is therefore an important supplement in your diet.

In powder or liquid form, mix one tablespoon with water or add to fresh vegetable juice. Use only chlorella that is extracted from alfalfa or other plants; avoid the chemically extracted variety. In tablet form, chew a few at the end of meals with a little food. This reduces the desire to eat sweets later. Tablets also go well at other times of the day to quell blood sugar rushes and the associated craving, either alone or with a snack such as roasted pumpkin seeds or celery sticks. (Chlorella tablets must be thoroughly chewed or they will not digest fully.) Any residue on the teeth or gums will protect and heal those tissues of the mouth. (Refer to the Resources chapter for best quality Chlorella.)

PART 6 ~ HOW TO PLAN YOUR MEALS

Vitality! That's the pursuit of life, isn't it?"
—Katherine Hepburn—

P lanning a daily menu is simply a matter of common sense and a touch of intuition. Serve vegetables with a grain for complete nourishment, light foods with heavy ones, and sweet foods with sour ones. Weather conditions should also be considered. On hot days, raw foods are cooling; on cold days, cooked foods provide warmth.

Organize your meal for the next day by soaking a grain overnight. For practicality sake, measure enough grain for two dishes. For example: Armenian Couscous for lunch and Blueberry Couscous Cake for the evening dessert; Brown Rice and Sesame Salt for lunch, and Vegetable Stir-Fried Rice for dinner.

PRESENTATION
Presentation is also part of the eating experience. A colorful meal stimulates the taste buds, dazzles the eyes, and encourages a healthy appetite. To visually enliven a solitary colored dish such as puréed soup or sauce, add a garnish with a contrasting color such as a sprig of cilantro. For another visual dimension, use colorful plates and bowls that compliment the food.

Center each meal around a grain and serve it in a separate bowl to signify its importance. Then, instead of plating each meal, share your food by placing all other dishes in the center of the table.

TRAVELWISE
When traveling to other climates, gradually prepare your body for the change. A few days before you leave, include foods in your diet that are grown in that region and prepare them according to what is appropriate for that climate: raw and lightly cooked for warm climates; long simmered for cold climates.

TIPS ON EATING OUT
Refined sugar, oil, and salt are prevailing ingredients from fast food chains to five-star restaurants. So making conscious choices means asking conscious questions. Here are some basic tips that will help your dining experience be a healthy one.

* Study the menu. It reveals all the ingredients in the kitchen. If a dish is prepared to order, you can ask the chef to eliminate unhealthy ingredients or substitute healthier ones.

- Often our best choices are the appetizers and side dishes that accompany the main courses. A few of these could serve as your main course.

- If choosing fish, ask which are wild caught and which are farm raised. Always choose wild caught.

- Order broiled instead of fried; skip the bread and desserts; and instead of alcohol, order sparkling spring water with lemon or lime slices.

- Be cautious when ordering soups. Ask what ingredients are used. Bean and lentil soups are sometimes prepared with pork, while the base for cream soups can be heavy cream, evaporated milk, or other canned dairy products.

- No prepared dressings. To be on the safe side, carry the basics with you—sea salt and oil. You can then easily make your own salad dressing along with lemons from the kitchen. This dressing also serves as a healthy substitute for butter on a baked potato.

- Many of the dishes served in Oriental and Thai restaurants include sugar and MSG. For example, sushi rice is prepared with sugar; and although the ingredients in the dish may not be prepared with sugar or MSG, the bottled sauces such as soy and Hoisan cooked into the dish may contain these and other chemical ingredients.

Each of us can make a difference in the quality of food served in our restaurants. Critique the meal according to both its taste and health aspects and let the chef know. If enough patrons request conscious cookery, restaurateurs will respond.

FOOD FOR THOUGHT

Set aside a special time and place for meals in a clean environment surrounded with pleasant sounds and conversation.

Cook with friends or family. Some of the most meaningful conversations happen over the preparation of food.

Teach your children how to cook.

Cooking brings gratification, satisfaction, and communion and is one of life's greatest simple pleasures.

At mealtime, cast off care and anxious thought; do not feel hurried, but eat slowly and with cheerfulness, with your heart filled with gratitude for the blessing of life.

Food is our highest medicine

PART 7 ~ RESOURCES

"If you have integrity, nothing else matters.
If you don't have integrity, nothing else matters."
—Alan Simpson—

Part 7: Resources

The companies listed below maintain the highest standards and a dedication to providing best quality products and services.

Macrobiotic products—Listings can include miso, mochi, tamari, shoyu, umeboshi products, sea vegetables, soba and udon noodles, brown rice vinegar, brown rice mirin, kuzu, sesame salt (gomasio), brown rice syrup, and barley malt syrup.

- ★ Eden Foods—Full line of macrobiotic foods; sesame and olive oils; soymilk selection; whole grain pasta; beans in BPA-free lined cans; snacks; and over 250 authentic, organic, kosher pure foods; 888.424.3336; edenfoods.com

- ★ Kushi Institute—Full line of macrobiotic products and kitchen tools; 800.975.8744; kushiinstitute.org

- ★ Naturally Selina—Vegan/raw/gluten-free; macrobiotic, stevia powder; health and beauty aids, kitchen tools, and much more; 800.867.7258; naturallyselina.com

- ★ Celtic Sea Salt—Unprocessed, kosher sea salt from pristine coastal regions; high mineral Hawaiian and Portuguese sea salts; organic black pepper; roasted sesame salts w/grinder; 800.867.7258; celticseasalt.com

- ★ Clean Water Revival (CWR)—Water and air filtration products from portable units to sophisticated water filtration systems including the Doulton water filters of England; 800.444.3563; cwrenviro.com
  (*Use the Promo Code STOMACH, for a 5% discount on all products.*)

- ★ Essential Living Foods—Organic: yacon syrup and yacon powder; coconut sugar, coconut nectar, coconut water powder; hemp seeds, chia seeds, wild crafted sacha inchi nuts; sacha inchi oil and raw coconut oil; Ceylon red rice; cacao products; goji berry; spirulina, spices
  310.319.1555; essentiallivingfoods.com
  (*Use the Promo Code HAPPYSTOMACH, for a 5% discount on all products.*)

- Kitchen Craft Waterless Cookware—828.707.1281; healthycookingconcepts.com

- Prime Chlorella Co.—Purest chlorella products, cultured in filtered clean mineral water, and processed especially for highest digestion; 888.277.7330 or 403.932.8990; primechlorella.com

- Stevia.com—Stevia concentrate dark liquid; 301.823.9559; stevia.com (HealthWorld Online)

- The Palm Beach Cookie—Diabetic friendly and totally organic; 561.601.9683; thepalmbeachcookie.com

HEALING HOLIDAY RETREAT

HappyStomach Retreat—Jan London offers a unique healing experience on one of Panama's Caribbean islands.
Eat beautiful food created especially for you; join in edifying cooking classes and discussions or activities such as snorkeling, surfing, cayuco sailing, yoga, and nature walks; and sleep peacefully by the sea while you restore your health effortlessly.

Jan also offers dietary counseling and menu planning via skype or email.
For further information, contact Jan at: info@happystomachretreat.com

MEASUREMENTS AND METRIC CONVERSIONS

Dry measurements		
¼ teaspoon	4 grams	
½ teaspoon	7 grams	
1 teaspoon	5 grams	
1 tablespoon	14 grams	
½ ounce	2 tablespoons	15 grams
4 ounce	½ cup	113 grams
1 tablespoon	3 teaspoons	

Liquid measurements		
1 teaspoon	5 milliliters	
3 tablespoons	¼ cup	59 ml
½ cup	188 ml	
1 cup	22 grams	
1 quart	¼ gallon	1.1 liters

Weight equivalents	
1 ounce	28.35 grams
1 pound	16 ounces
1 pound	453 grams

Oven temperatures	
300°F	150°C
325°F	160°C
350°F	180°C

Approximate equivalents	
1 cup flour	100 grams
1 tablespoon oil	14 grams
1 tablespoon water	15 grams

INDEX

Note: Main references are printed in **bold type**. References to Dash of Wisdom are printed in ***bold italic***, best recipes for a particular food item are printed in *italic* type. Not all instances of an ingredient in a recipe are indexed.

Food is our highest medicine

Food is our highest medicine

RECIPE LOCATOR

Grains and noodles

Land vegetables

Soups

Dishes

Legumes

Savory sauces and dressings

NOTES

Eat and be happy!

Food is our highest medicine